Seljuk Cuisine

Published by Blue Dome Press
244 5th Avenue, Suite D-149
New York, NY 10001, USA

www.bluedomepress.com

Art Director Engin Çiftçi
Graphic Design Nurdoğan Çakmakçı - İbrahim Akdağ
Photographs Semih Ural

C 41.595

ISBN: 978-1-935295-54-9

Printed by
Imak Ofset, Istanbul - Turkey

Seljuk Cuisine

A Chef's Quest for His Soulmate

M. Ömür Akkor

New York

Contents

Preface

I always felt close to the Seljuks; their mathematics, art and lifestyle always caught my attention. During a trip to Beyşehir, I found myself absorbed in a story belonging to the Seljuk period.

In addition to being written on the subject of what was eaten during the Seljuk period, this book also animates the Seljuks' way of life and the story in it brings to life a plot belonging to that age.

Other artists contributed to the story, too. Suzan Çataloluk gave life to the book with miniatures from that period, and İbrahim Kuşlu gave new life to ceramic tiles from that time. I hope that through their beautiful artwork, through reading recipes from that period, and through actually eating the food they ate, you might feel a little bit like a Seljuk, too.

The book is comprised of three sections. In the first section, you will read a story by a chef working in Kubadabad Palace. In the second section, there is a story told by a chef of this age. In the final section, you will find recipes from the Seljuks.

In regard to the recipes of Seljuk cuisine, it would be a great mistake to say, is this all? But when the conditions of that time are thought about and the shortage of written sources is taken into consideration, it should be understood that I have set out from a very small point in regard to the sources at hand and recipes were written accordingly. Although some of the recipes included in this book are found in books from that period, some of them only have a name or contents remaining. At this point I would like to indicate that I have benefited from my intuition, which has developed from my experience as a chef and from my work directed towards understanding the food of the Hittites when I was a part of the Alacahöyük excavation work.

My goal is to open another window to the depth of the Turkish culinary culture and to shed light on what was eaten during those centuries and the history of the food that we eat today. I hope that my work will increase interest in Seljuk cuisine and will be a vehicle for researchers to work in this field.

M. Ömür Akkor

Acknowledgments

I would like to thank the following: My teachers İbrahim İ. Öztahtalı and Zeki Gürdal Karaoğlu for enabling the story to take a very different state and for their fellowship; Ibrahim Kuşlu for giving life to my book with his ceramic tiles; Suzan Çataloluk for relating my story and the period with miniatures from that time; Semih Ural for his splendid photographs; and Haluk Sönmezer for completing the book with his designs. During the development and writing of the book and the period of finding sources for it, I saw unconditional support from: my valuable teachers at the Seljuk University Ali Akkanat Vocational School and the Seljuk University Konya Campus; Elvin Otman, a teacher from the Bilkent University History Department; my valuable sister, Zennup Pınar Çakmakcı, who read and corrected time and again every recipe and every page and who has made at least as much effort as I have from the inception of this book, and her esteemed husband, Ramazan Çakmakcı; Nevin Halıcı, an important author on Turkish Culinary Culture, whose books I benefited from during the period of determining the book's recipes and from whom I received ideas in many places during the writing of the book; my valued co-workers at the Bademiçi Restaurant who never refused help during the shooting of photographs, Yücel Erdemir, Sevim Üstünbostancı, Selahattin Tetik, Şahin Tetik, Veysel Varhan, Emre İdrisoğlu, Özlem Koçak, Barış Paçacı, Sezer Ormancı, Orhan Mutlu and Nazik Kaymak; my esteemed teacher Tevfik Türkyılmaz and his family; my mother Cevriye Bilgici, my father Doğan Akkor and my twin brother Yunus Emre Akkor, who were always at my side; and the Doğan family, which is my second family in Bursa. I thank each of them very much and I think that if one of them was not there, this book would not have come about.

To Lara Uğurlu, who will always live like the chef in the story. "This is such a place that the more you stay the more it grows and broadens and becomes infinite. I felt like I was a kernel of wheat in the vast Konya plain. At times the wind blew me about, but I could not go far."

Section I

1236

Bath tiles, Kubadabad Palace (13ᵗʰ century)

The Longest April

Spring comes late to Konya ...

I never knew why I was here, and this never made me uncomfortable. Ever since I started thinking this was contentment, I have never even gone outside the dervish lodge. I was supposed to prepare the soup this morning. First I lit the stove and waited there a little. When my chill passed, I went to the pantry and got some supplies.

In this place where I did not even remember my past, was I content only because I cooked or was it the profound and silent contentment of green Konya that held me here?

How long have I been here? What have I seen? I had forgotten everything. This strange peace encompassed me more and more, and I remained longer and longer. Finally I had decided not to leave. My whole world had become here. This was such a place that the longer you stay, the more it grew and broadened and became infinite. I felt like I was a kernel of wheat in the vast Konya plain. At times the wind blew me about, but I could not go far. As all these things were passing through my mind, somehow I found myself in the pantry, and here everything was happening like this!

From the pantry, I took two spoons of roasted meat, two onions, and a bowl of bulgur, chickpeas, beans and green lentils that I had soaked overnight. I returned to the kitchen to make tandoor soup.

I put the broth I had left next to the stove last night before the fire went out back on the top of the stove and added the pulses. I put the meat cured last winter with the finely chopped onion and left them to cook over the fire.

The raw food cooked as it heated up and became better as it cooked. At that moment, I thought of myself; perhaps life was as simple as cooking and perhaps that was the reason I had stayed in Konya this long. My master would say that "making food is a station." Without any hurrying, I had waited for months to be able to make soup.

Seljuk plate (13th century)

A Quiet Afternoon

The rare bustle at the dervish lodge was over. Life continued with its everyday calm. Spring came late to Konya, but the warmth of April was unique. While I was sitting in front of the kitchen, the door suddenly opened and the Sheikh of the dervish lodge appeared. He had left at the morning call-to-prayer and returned at the *Asr* (Afternoon Prayer). He said, "Water."

I immediately went to the kitchen and filled a glass with water. Perhaps he might want to drink sherbet, so I put *Sirkencübin* in another glass. I quietly approached his door and, bending over, I left the tray on the floor.

Just as I was leaving his room he said, "If the honey and vinegar are in equal proportion, it becomes delicious; don't forget," he said.

Indistinctly saying "all right" with my inner voice, I disappeared from the door. Going to the pantry, I returned to the kitchen with vinegar and honey. I put the honey, vinegar, and water into a copper bowl in the proportions the Sheikh had said and mixed them together with a wooden spoon. I dipped my ladle in and drank until I quenched my thirst. It was as if a winter as cold as ice had taken the place of the early April warmth. I don't know how much I drank, but I had found the right measurement. Like my Sheikh had said, one to one.

Seljuk bowl (13th century)

The Old Day and New Day

I had learned the real measurements of the sherbet. Had the time come? Or had my time come? Why had it been said now? OK, feeling that my time had come, how did I put a glass of sherbet next to the water? Or how had I surmised this? If I had missed that moment, when would I be told the essential measurement? I thought about these all evening; I was unable to sleep.

This was one of the things that tired me most in the dervish lodge. I would try and extract meanings from the silence, the identity of which could not be understood. This was perhaps my favorite game. Now I needed to sleep. The next morning I was going to get up early and buy provisions from the women's bazaar. Just across from the dervish lodge, the bazaar was the place I liked to visit most in Konya—at any rate, I didn't go anyplace else—you should have seen the festival of colors. If it weren't for the bazaar, I would never leave the dervish lodge. Perhaps the wheat-stalk's height extended only this far.

I don't know how long I slept, but regardless of how long you sleep on a wooden bench, the same hardness wakes you up. Due a little to morning grogginess and a little to the cold, I got up with great difficulty. Saying it's a new April morning, I washed my face with the water in the copper bucket and went to the kitchen.

Yunus, who had come to the dervish lodge last year, had prepared the soup. This was my favorite soup—*tutmaç* soup; it was exactly like a feast.

The day was going to be good. The sun had long since begun to shine. I am sure that the vegetables at the bazaar would be unbelievable. For this reason, I like spring, summer and autumn the best. The faces smiling together with the light of the sun, and the variety of the bazaar would be added to them.

Saying, "Yunus, health to your hands," I left the dervish lodge.

Even though I describe the dervish lodge as though I were alone, actually we were many. It was the silence that showed us to be few.

With the sun on my back, I walked towards the bazaar. Konya had awakened with me and was on the streets. Some of the vendors had come and set up their stands; some were just coming. It was the best time of the bazaar; everything had just been arranged and everything was very fresh. All the busyness was silent. Actually it was not the dervish order, but it was Konya that was silent.

Greens were lined up on the first stand I saw; the smell of the soil in their roots was unbelievable. Sellers of cheese, bread, yogurt, vegetables. The bazaar was a different realm.

I was weighed down so much after all my purchases that I almost couldn't walk, but my eyes were still looking for molded cheese that I had not been able to get. Thinking that I'd get it the next time, I returned to the dervish lodge.

Everything Is Upside-Down

My master was in the kitchen; taking permission, I approached him. Before entering the kitchen, the call, "Permission, O Sufis!" would be made; the kitchen would be entered only when permission was granted from inside. The kitchen was the most sacred place in the dervish lodge. It was believed that there was an eternal spirit there and that the spirit did not want to be disturbed, so there was never a lack of respect.

Today a meat dish would be made because it was sacred Friday. Meat was only cooked on Fridays. Friday dinner! If you cooked with the master on Friday, that meant you "had arrived." New apprentices were not allowed in the kitchen on Fridays. Just as I was about to leave after dropping off the things I had brought from the bazaar, my master said, "Stop!" Or ...

If a new soul wanted to come to the dervish lodge, he would stand at the side on a sheepskin for three days in the kitchen and observe us. If he was to continue, he would run errands for eighteen days in his own clothing.

If he passed this stage, kitchen uniforms would be given to him at the end of the eighteenth day.

After this, a trial would begin that would continue for exactly one-thousand and one days. Patience would be tested with tasks that were repeated again and again. For patience was the dervish lodge's basic principle. The basic principle of the trial was to accept everything as it is. Then obedience and finally attitude would be tested. Sometimes, those who understood they could not endure this would "break-off the trial" and escape from the dervish lodge.

I was next to my master, Yusuf. There were some eggplants, plums, and meat on the wooden table. As much as I understood from the ingredients, he was going to make crock kebab. My master said, "Hurry and begin by cutting the heads off the eggplants." Or had I reached the level?

I finished the job he gave me with great enthusiasm. I was waiting at the side with the contentment of the felicity I had met. My master said, "Don't stand far off; come close to the stove." We were going to put the food on the stove when I realized that the wood was finished, so I turned towards the door to bring wood in from outside. My master said, "Wait." When I turned towards my master, there were several pieces of wood in his lap. My Friday dinner ... Thankfulness ... The smell of the crock kebab had filled the whole kitchen.

The dinner tray was ready on the floor; in front of everyone, there was a wooden spoon turned upside-down, a pinch of salt and three slices of bread. The food was put in the middle and before beginning to eat, everyone wet his right index finger with his tongue and then put his finger in the salt. He began eating by licking the salt and finished in the same way.

Food was eaten from a common dish in the middle, but while eating, a person would not put the whole spoon in his mouth. As if the spoon had been divided in two lengthwise, a person would bring half the spoon to his lips and put the half that had not touched his lips into the food.

Everyone was well-mannered at the table and never spoke. If someone wanted to drink water, he would signal the person waiting on foot; after kissing the glass of water, the waiter would extend it to the person who wanted it. The person who asked for the water would take the glass and after kissing it, he would drink the water. No one would eat while this was happening, so no one infringed upon another's rights.

I got up after the Prayer; I was going to read a little from a religious treatise when my master Yusuf, also known as Saint of Cooks, said, "To the garden," and silently went out from the door. He walked towards the rose-garden and sat on a rock at the edge of the garden. You cannot imagine what passed through my mind during this short walk. Or had I made a mistake?

After a long silence he said, "You're going; get ready."

It was as if the dervish lodge had fallen on top of me. What did "Get ready" mean for a man who had nothing but a sheepskin he slept on? What did I have? Nothing ... Where could I go? No place ... As if my whole life had not passed in this dervish lodge. Where else was there to go? No place ... I stood still without asking anything. I was frozen before my master. When I woke up this morning, the toe of my shoe was not showing the door. Or I had not been called to the back door. When someone was not wanted in the dervish lodge, he would be sent away by these two means. Well, now in the middle of the rose-garden, where was I going? And more importantly, what should I prepare for?

A Journey

Sultan Kayqubad was going to move into his newly constructed summer palace Kubadabad in May. I was to go to the palace kitchen.

Everything was this easy and, at the same time, this difficult.

No one had gone to the palace from the dervish lodge before, so why was I going? Ever since I left the rose-garden, my mind had been totally confused. I would go, but my mind would remain here. That night, my old wooden cot hurt my back more than ever. I didn't sleep even a moment. My preparations should not take long, because I had to go immediately. It would be more difficult to go if more time lapsed. I had to set out on my journey within two days.

Had my training at this dervish lodge come to an end? If it had, why should I go to a palace? Was there no place else to go?

I awoke from my sleepless sleep. After washing my hands and face, I went out into the courtyard. Many years of my life had passed here. This place had been my mother, father, beloved, homeland, yearning, reunion, and family. I thought of these things. The more I thought, the more I felt saddened; the sadder I felt, the more I thought.

A leaf fell gently from a tree. The fallen leaf belonged to that tree; who could change that? Even if it was on the ground, it belonged to the tree.

I belonged to this dervish lodge; regardless of where I went, nothing could change this. Even if no one saw it, its print was in my heart. I felt a little better. When I turned around, my master was there. "Even if water flows backwards a few days, it will certainly return to its own bed with goodness," he said, and he put a small piece of paper in the palm of my hand. Without looking, without being able to look at what was in my palm, I put it in my sash.

He cautioned that he would give a dinner for me in the evening and that for this reason I should go to the bazaar before it got late. Perhaps this meant to go and see the bazaar for a last time since my fate was not clear.

Was the bazaar quieter this morning? Or did it just seem that way to me? I was burning inside; I had been cooked, at any rate. Were we going to eat a meal as well? I returned to the kitchen like a vagabond. We were going to make the preparations all together.

My master said, "*Belh* rice and honey halva are to be made." We prepared the ingredients, and everyone was in the kitchen. We were to spend our last time together. We were many, but we extended the work. There was still a lot of time until evening, and we were dallying. The whole day passed in this way. When a person knows he will go, he cannot hold on to time. It passes faster. We had begun to cook. While the rice was being prepared, halva was being cooked at the same time. The kitchen smelled amazing.

My master came and said, "Dinner will be eaten in the guest hall." Who was this guest?

The Sheikh of our dervish lodge was also going to attend this meal. Who was this guest?

Low wooden tables were set up and sheepskins were spread. Sheikh, my master, and I sat next to one another. But there was no guest. This silence, this evening meal, this distinction filled my eyes with tears. I met eye-to-eye with the Sheikh; he said "I hope all is well," and smiled. At last I understood. I was the guest. And I was being sent off from here in a fitting way.

I went to my room. I fell asleep reading. When I woke up at the morning call-to-prayer, everyone else was up. I got ready; even my sheepskin was going to remain here. I was to join a caravan at the south gate of the city and arrive on horseback at Beyşehir in the evening. The caravan's man and my horse stood in front of the dervish lodge. I said farewell to everyone from the dervish lodge and we mutually forgave one another for any wrong that might have been done to one another. I asked permission from the Sheikh and, kissing the hand of my master, I left. Let me tell you something; I knew as certainly that I know my name that I would never return to Konya. This journey was such a journey.

> "Morning sun,
> April coolness,
> My bay horse...
> I am centuries away from my past and future."

Everything I had remained behind. This was the first time I had been so far from the city. When I looked behind, Konya was standing in the middle of an infinite plain. How small it looked in my eyes. I raised my right hand and gave a salute. "Goodbye, Konya," I said. Suddenly I remembered the piece of paper my master had squeezed into my hand ... I took into my hand the piece of paper that I had tucked into my sash without knowing what it was. I slowly unfolded it and looked. What was written here? Nothing ... I gently folded this trust of my master and put it in its place.

We stopped much later for a water break. We were close to Beyşehir. The April sun warmed, but didn't burn. I got off my horse. I felt excited and this surprised me; why was I excited? I took out my loaf of bread and ate it. Actually, I was very hungry. When the caravan foreman said to mount, we set off once again. My excitement was steadily increasing. We passed through a small valley and suddenly there were green waters in front of me. At that moment I truly thought for the first time, "Nothing will ever be the same." The green that had been the dervish lodge's contentment for years, the green that drives one crazy, the green that spoils contentment and becomes contentment was before me for the first time. I froze in my footsteps; it was as if life stood still and I could proceed no more. I had remained in the moment I had first seen the water. Where was this place?

After walking at the edge of the lake for a while, we came to Beyşehir and the palace appeared. The palace extended from the top of a hill to the edge of the lake.

The head of the caravan said to me, "Go and find the head butler at the palace."

I turned over my horse and walked to the gate of the palace. I told the soldier there that I had come from the dervish lodge and that I wanted to see the head butler. Together with the soldier, we went to another gate. I said the same thing there. Then to another gate and then another gate ... After four successive interchanges, I was at the door of the head butler.

What kind of business was this? At the dervish lodge, anyone who wanted to see the Sheikh would knock on his door, ask for permission, and enter. What kind of order was this? I was amazed by the crowd. A little later, the doorman called me and I finally entered inside. I reached my target behind door after door.

He said that they would show me where to stay, that I would get accustomed to the kitchen here in a few days, and that later on he would again tell me what was necessary. Calling the room servant, he ordered him to show me a suitable room and then to take me to the kitchen.

When I stepped out onto the stone courtyard, the sun had descended very low and everywhere had become wrapped in red. We walked from the courtyard towards the Small Palace in front. The kitchen was in the Upper Palace, and the place I was to stay was in the Lower Palace. We walked from the Lower Palace's courtyard past the stairs and came to a small terrace. The terrace faced the lake. After passing through the side door, we were immediately in a service corridor where small rooms were located. Opening the wooden door at the end of the corridor, the room servant said, "This is your room; after you have settled in there is food in the kitchen next to your terrace. Stay there and later the kitchen service will find you," and he left.

Four stone walls, a closet and, surprisingly, a bed on the floor. My window looked out to the terrace and the lake beyond it.

Amazed by this unequaled scenery after the walls of my dervish lodge in Konya, I went out to the terrace. I walked down the stone steps towards the lake. The sun had become scarlet and was on top of the mountains across from me. There was a small wooden dock at the edge of the lake, and I walked towards it. "I'll watch the sunset and then go to the kitchen," I thought. Bending over the edge of the dock, I looked into the water. It had maybe been months since I had seen my face. The turban on my head, my beard and my pale face were rippling on top of the water. Who knows, perhaps my rippling reflection would remain in the waters for centuries.

I was suddenly startled by the voice, "Dervish, *hu*!"

The same voice asked, "Are you the one who came from Konya?"

I turned around; someone my height and a little overweight was calling to me with a smile. In amazement I said, "Yes, I have come from Konya. My name is Umar."

Smiling, the man across from me said, "I am Jalabi; I work in the kitchen. Come and we'll eat dinner together and I will tell you about this place."

Jalabi became my closest friend as long as I stayed at the palace.

We entered the dining hall; there was a lot of commotion—talking, shouting, laughing- everyone was having a good time. The most distracting thing in that crowd was my silence.

"Get accustomed to this," Jalabi said. Then he called to the dervish on duty, "Bring us some food." A few minutes later some plates, a pitcher and wooden spoons came to the table.

When Jalabi said, "Bring some barley bread," I couldn't restrain myself. "Are we going to eat all of these?" I asked.

"What is there on the table?" he questioned. I was dumbfounded. "Soup, food, dessert, sherbet and barley bread. I wasn't even hosted like this when I left the dervish lodge."

"This is a palace not a dervish lodge," he said. "Thirty sheep are slaughtered every day in the kitchen here," he continued. "We eat whatever our Sultan, Ala ad-Din Kayqubad, eats. May God not allow his health to decline." At the same, time he was chewing the bites of food he was snacking on.

As I thought about our only eating meat on Fridays at the dervish lodge, our eating only one variety of food at a meal, and our table manners, I felt that I had come to hell rather than a palace.

Jalabi continued non-stop. "You have to get used to it; time doesn't pass here just by thinking. Next week our Illustrious Sultan will visit the palace and there is a banquet for the opening of the palace. After that, the month of Ramadan is coming. As you see, there is a lot to be done; don't tire yourself for nothing with thinking. You haven't even taken a spoonful of food yet. Why don't you start eating, Umar, there won't be anything left later on!" Saying this, he continued eating.

How would I get used to this commotion? At the end of dinner, we went out on the terrace. "I'll tell the butler; if you come to me in the kitchen tomorrow morning, we'll begin work. I'm going home," he said. Surprised, I asked, "Home?"

Jalabi said, "Yes, yes. I live in the village below; I don't stay at the palace." Saying goodbye, he left, making remarks right and left.

I began to walk towards my room. Remembering the religious treatise in my pocket, it passed through my mind that I would both read and sleep early. When I lit two candles and sat on my bed, I was astonished. My bed, my quilt and my pillow were all wool; I was going to sleep in a palace.

With the treatise in my hand, I fell into a deep sleep.

Bath tiles, Kubadabad Palace (13th century)

First Days

We were up to our necks in work in the kitchen. Sultan Kayqubad had come to his summer palace and the opening banquet was to take place tomorrow. The whole city and also prominent people of Konya were invited. If I told myself that I had become accustomed to my new place, I was too tired to listen. Actually, I didn't even know if I had become accustomed or not.

Maybe this was better. Although Jalabi had caused me concern initially, he was a good man. It was a good thing that he was at the palace and we had become friends.

The head butler had brought the menu a day earlier. The list of food to be prepared for the opening banquet was as follows:

Pomegranate Sherbet (Nardenk Şerbeti)

Honey Sherbet with Lemon (Limonlu Bal Şerbeti)

Snow Sherbet (Kar Şerbeti)

Liver Soup (Ciğer Çorbası)

Rice with pepper

Pit Roasted Lamb (Biryan)

Roasted Lamb (Ateşte Kuzu)

Roasted Chicken (Söğülme Tavuk)

Partridge or Quail on Skewers (Şişte Keklik ya da Bıldırcın)

Halva with Pine Nuts (Fıstıklı Helva)

Flour Halva (Un Helvası)

Memnuniye Halva (Memnuniye)

Flat Kataifi (Yassı Kadayıf)

I had not been able to leave the kitchen for a day. In the kitchen we were all tied to the head butler, but every unit we worked in had its own head: like the head halva-maker, head sherbet-maker, and head pilaf-maker. In order to learn every job, we worked under all the masters.

Generally, Jalabi and I always worked under the same master; we both prepared food and talked over our troubles. I was going to make delight and Jalabi was going to make flour halva. We got all the ingredients together and were going to cook the halva the next morning. Everything was ready for the next day. We were going to cook the halva in pans as tall as men.

On banquet days, the kitchen was transported to the garden, and meat was left to cook over wood fires lit at night. There were a thousand kinds of aromas in the palace courtyard. Plates, bowls, wooden tables—every place became a kitchen.

While the Sultan dined with his guests at a table prepared on his own terrace, the food was put into gold and ceramic dishes. I had grown to like Kubadabad. The ceramics played a very big role in this. The most important artisans of the time made their most beautiful works for this palace. The ceramic tiles in the palace walls took their color from the lake. The artisans must have wanted to make a reflection, for the color of the lake embraced all sides. Sometimes I would remain in front of these ceramic walls; I couldn't help but gaze at them for a long time. The designs were unique—fish, birds and trees. I could not even guess where this power of imagination had come from. Maybe these ceramic tiles helped me to distract myself after the dervish lodge. The ceramic plates, bowls and pitchers put before the Sultan were distinctly beautiful. The table was very colorful with the gold objects and ceramic works.

From time to time I thought that if I had not prepared food, I would probably have been a ceramic-maker. While all these thoughts were passing through my mind, I was startled by Jalabi's voice: "Again you are day-dreaming, dervish; are you still at the dervish lodge?"

"No, Jalabi, no," I replied. "My life has turned from simplicity into commotion. I am amazed as to how I have gotten used to all these things. While the dervish lodge is still silent, always the same and fixed, how am I in a life like this? I guess I am forgetting the life I came from, and this frightens me," I said.

"Why would you fear this life? Is it bad that we are in it? You are making too much out of it," Jalabi said.

I was sad that I had made him sad. "Don't get upset; I didn't mean that," I retorted.

He replied, "It's late. If your work is finished, go get some rest and we will meet early tomorrow morning in the kitchen." I slowly retreated to my room. The treatise in my pocket remained the same as it came; I took it out and put it under my pillow. I put out the gas lantern and stretched out on my bed.

I was in the kitchen early in the morning. Everyone was taking their halva pot and putting it over a fire in place of the meat. Placing the halva pot over the fire, I took the semolina and butter, and began cooking the halva.

Almost no food remained from the great banquet. My arm was about to drop off from stirring halva with a wooden spoon for the whole day. Jalabi was in the same situation. I was off the next day after this tiring event.

I hadn't understood much from this situation. While thinking, *What am I going to do on my day off,* Jalabi said, "Come to the village below, tomorrow on your day off. We'll go to the bazaar and eat together." I was surprised.

"Should we go around?" I asked.

"Yes, you haven't seen the village since you came; it will do you good," he replied. "Come before breakfast and we'll meet at the village bazaar," he added.

When I asked, "How will I find the bazaar, Jalabi," he laughed and said, "It's set up in the square; you'll find it." We were going to meet after dawn.

I woke up early the next morning. I walked down to the edge of the lake, moving through the morning quiet. I hadn't had the time to even look at the water for days. After passing row-boat shelters and small shops, I arrived at the bazaar. It had long since been set up. The bazaar had a lot of variety and it was colorful; I liked the roving food-sellers the best. Vegetables and fruit, on the one hand, and food, on the other hand. While looking around at the tables, I saw that Jalabi had come.

"I guess you understand why I told you to come before eating," he said.

"Yes, I understand," I replied.

"What shall we eat? There is a seller of sheep's head and a seller of trotters; there's no *herise* (meat paste) at this time. When the head and trotters are finished, there is *tirit* (bread soaked in gravy) in the bazaar. In other words, sheep's head and trotters in the morning. *Tirit* and *herise* at noon," he said.

"Let's have trotters then," I suggested.

Jalabi said to one of the roving food-sellers, "Trotters-seller Ramadan, give me two of them." Ramadan put the trotters in two copper bowls and extended some bread.

"May it benefit you, sir," he said.

27

Jalabi extended the *akçe* he took from his pocket to Ramadan. "Oh, by the way, this money pouch is yours," he said and gave it to me.

When I looked at his face thinking, *What is this Jalabi?* he said, "This is a palace not a dervish lodge; did you forget that, Umar?"

After we ate, we continued looking at the stands. The bazaar was small, but it had everything: sellers of herbs, honey, rice, figs, water, oil, vinegar, sugar, halva, brooms, dishes, water jugs, baskets, knives. And much more …

After walking around the bazaar, we went down to the edge of the lake. Before us stood a rising fortress on an island in the lake. I asked, "Does this fortress belong to the palace?"

"Yes, it was made to protect the palace, but there was a secret passage connecting this fortress to the palace," he said.

"Wow!" I replied. So there must have been a road under the water. What lengths are taken for protection from harm, I thought. The dervish lodge, the print of which I always carried in my heart, came to mind: in the middle of Konya, its door was always open. No precaution was taken to protect it from harm. If you wanted to do something, you could, but once you entered the door of the lodge, the Sheikh's fire enveloped you. Even if you didn't see anything, you knew that. The door to evil was always closed.

I said, "May God close everyone's door to evil." He said, "Amen" and continued, "It's noon so let's go to my house; I'm getting hungry again."

I replied, "OK, is your house nearby?"

"There is a small market area after the bazaar; it's at the end of the market area," he said.

We passed through the bazaar again; the smell of *herise* was everywhere. The market was on the other edge of the bazaar. It was like a square comprised of five or six shops around a fountain. When we reached the square, there were shops like those of the baker, sweets-seller and cloth-seller. Suddenly, I thought about going to the halva-seller. "Jalabi, come here," I said, and I entered the confectionary.

In addition to glass jars of almond candy, *nebet* (crystallized sugar) candy and *akide* (sugar) candy, there was also walnut and almond halva. In addition, there was also raw sugar found here like the sugar we used for sweets in the palace. Extending the money pouch from my pocket, I said, "Would you give me a little candy?" but, smiling, Jalabi interrupted:

"Hey dervish, you don't know about the *akçe*s; we could open a shop with the candy that this money can buy."

We would go to the bazaar at the dervish lodge, but we did not pay the money. They would come and get the money from the lodge. For this reason, I didn't know anything about exchanging money. Jalabi said, "First ask the price and then give the money." I told him OK.

The candy-seller put the candy into a package. I paid him and we left the candy shop. "Let's also get some bread from the bakery," Jalabi said.

We bought ten loaves of flatbread from the bakery and started to the house.

Pushing the wooden door, we entered the courtyard. The overhead grapevines had covered the whole courtyard. This one-storey house surrounded the edge of the courtyard with its tiny rooms.

"We're here!" shouted Jalabi. "Set the table!" he continued.

We went to the sitting room just across from the gate. There was a large room with cushions on the floor. The low wooden table was at the side. Jalabi pulled the table in front of us.

I tried to remember my family. I couldn't even remember when I had eaten with my family last. How lucky he is, I thought. He can eat with his family at the same table every evening. The worldly things I had forgotten slowly came to mind. If I had not become involved in this life, I would never know and remember them. Had I begun to forget my life at the dervish lodge?

Within an indeterminate period of time, the door opened and a copper tray was brought in. I didn't look to see who had brought the tray until it was placed in front of us on the table. Then I raised my head. Whose eyes had I encountered? Had my life, which stopped at the moment I first saw the lake, begun to advance now? I was startled again with the sentence, "My sister, Mahpari."

I had not even understood what this spring flying from these eyelashes and these deep lake-green eyes were. While passing all this through my mind, Mahpari had already left the room. "Let's begin, dervish," Jalabi said.

But I was not even in this world. I didn't know what this was. It was as if someone shot me in the heart and then left. Everything had begun to become meaningless. I didn't even understand what I ate. "Look, my mother made lentils and *borani* (stewed vegetables) for you," Jalabi said.

"Health to her hands," I replied uncertainly.

Now I wanted to immediately get up from the table and run away from here.

Which Love?

As soon as I left the house, I began to walk without knowing where I was going. I was very confused. Were Mahpari's eyes a sign of my doomsday? Had I completely deviated from the path? How could one look suffice for me to think of all these things? I only asked myself questions, but I could find no answers. Was this love? What was the love at the dervish lodge? Which one was real? Did they know all of this when they sent me from the lodge? Had they drawn my destiny when they chose to send me here? What would happen now? I passed the stone courtyard and went to my room. I immediately stretched out on my bed; it was as if I had gotten malaria. On the one hand, I was seeing nightmares and, on the other hand, I was talking in my sleep. My whole life had been turned upside-down. How could one look bring me to such a state? If Mahpari had spoken ... would I have died on the spot? Should I fear all of this? Or was love a good thing? I needed to try and calm down. If love were a bad thing, it would not be taught to us.

I spent the whole night in delirium. When the door to my room opened, I jumped out of bed in a sweat. It was Jalabi. I couldn't even look at his face. "Dervish? What happened to you?" he asked.

I couldn't even answer him. "You come to yourself and I'll bring you a bowl of soup," he said. I didn't want him to come at all. With difficulty, he had me drink a bowl of soup. He told me to lie down. He would tell the master and return to my side. Putting a pitcher of water at my side, he left.

I had begun to burn with love. If I drank all the water in the lake, this fire would not go out. Among all this regret, when would I see her again? Was I going to tell Jalabi? If I didn't see her again, what would happen?

Jalabi came again in the evening. I was burning in flames. He made me drink the herbs he had brought from the herbalist in a tea he had steeped. Later I fainted. In my dream, Mahpari walked across the waters of the lake to the island where the fortress was. "Come across the lake," she said. Just as I was about to put my foot in the water, I woke up.

I don't remember how much time had passed. But when morning came, my fever had fallen. I tried to get up from the bed, but I didn't have the strength. I opened the treatise under my pillow and began to read.

> Love,
> Burning both here and in the Hereafter.
> Love,
> As easy and as difficult as passing over the bridge to Paradise.
> Love,
> A disease that, if caught, cannot be abandoned.
> If it enters your blood,
> It becomes your past, your future, your sleep and your dreams.

Were these lines describing me? I got up from bed and went out to the courtyard. I couldn't even remember how many days I was in bed. Did all these things happen the day before or had days passed? The palace had not yet awoken. The silence in the courtyard calmed me down a little. I began to walk towards the upper kitchen. There were masters in the kitchen preparing the morning soup. I went to one of the cauldrons. I put a ladle of soup in a bowl and began to drink it. My stomach was growling from hunger.

Bath tiles, Kubadabad Palace (13th century)

I still had not found a satisfying answer. Would I be able to see Mahpari again? A little later the masters, began to come. Together with the masters, Jalabi and the head butler had also come.

While trying to understand why he had come, the head butler came to my side and said, "Dervish, you are going to make the Sultan's evening meal."

I was only able to ask, "Me?"

"Yes, you are going to make it. The Sultan said, 'Let the dervish make some food and I will eat it'," the head butler said.

When I asked, "Then what should I make?" he replied, "Are you asking me? You are the chef, Dervish; did you forget?" And then he disappeared from my side.

Well, what was I going to make now? Jalabi came to my side and asked, "What happened?"

"What could it be? I'm supposed to make the Sultan's dinner this evening, but I don't know what I'm going to make," I said.

"Don't worry," Jalabi said. "I'll help you."

While thinking about what I would make, Jalabi added, "Let's go to the pantry; we'll make something."

We got some ingredients from the pantry. I was going to prepare vermicelli with salted yogurt, chicken kebab, squash cooked with meat, and eggplant salad with vinegar, plus I was going to serve pickled turnips. I had not made the pickled turnips, but I had liked the taste of it very much.

The kitchen in the palace was very large. Each fireplace had a ventilator made from wood. There were wooden and stone counters, wire cupboards, wooden shelves, jars, and different size earthen bowls; the latter were sometimes used for cooking, sometimes to make pickles, cheese, or yogurt, and sometimes to store oil, honey, or grape molasses.

There were also many kinds of kitchen utensils. Trays, different sized bowls, jugs, and mortars from copper and ceramic; different sizes of cauldrons, pots, skillets, ladles, large wooden spoons, *bişkek*s for ayran, skewers and roasting spits for kebab, and much, much more. In addition, there were also stoves and ovens that sometimes burned with charcoal and sometimes with wood.

Oh, and there were kitchen uniforms.

In the kitchen, there were master chefs, their assistants, housekeepers, butlers, dishwashers and cleaners. On busy days, men would also come from outside to help; outside of the palace there were sellers of food like *biryan* kebab, bread, sherbet, halva, wheat pudding, head and trotters, and kebab, and there were butchers. If the chefs in the palace were not sufficient, food would be bought from them and they would make their food in the palace. On such days, we stayed by the master chefs and we would learn from them dishes we didn't know. Such days were training days for us.

Where was my mind roaming? The day had passed slowly. Dinner time was approaching. On one hand, I was cutting the meat and, on the other hand, I was trying to keep my mind busy.

"You're very quiet today," Jalabi said.

"I don't feel too well from the illness," I replied. Actually I still could not look him in the face. The evening meal had cleared my mind a little. Due to what I had experienced, I didn't want to think about anything for a few days. Plus my master had said:

A model of Seljuk ship with decorations

"Even if the water flows in the opposite direction for a few days

It will definitely return to its bed with goodness."

Thinking about this, I was trying to keep my mind calm. While I was washing the rice well and setting it aside, Jalabi began to brown the meat. The chicken I had rubbed with vinegar at noon had rested and I lit the charcoal stove to cook it.

The head butler's assistant came and asked about the food. "Everything will be ready before the evening call-to-prayer," I said.

I went to the other part of the kitchen to choose dishes. Before me, there were hundreds of porcelain plates, each different from and more beautiful than the others.

There I saw it for the first time.

It looked enchanting. Putting aside all the other plates in the kitchen, it was unique. While there were several of all the other plates, there was just one of this one. The color of the lake, fish, and plants were all on it. I was going to serve the main dish on it. I took the other plates haphazardly without choosing and went back to the food.

"Jalabi," I said, "I'm going to put the vegetables stewed with meat on this plate."

Leaving what was in his hands, he asked, "Why? What's special about it?"

"At least it is unique." I guess the plate had no importance for Jalabi. We put the dishes on a copper tray and the butler came. "You come too and wait at the door. If the Sultan likes the food, he will give you a purse of gold," he said.

Gold was not important, but still I would come. I was going to the top floors of the palace for the first time. From the kitchen, we went to the terrace, and from there to the Sultan's floor by means of the side stairs. When we came to the edge of the door of the entrance hall, the butler said, "You stay."

The head butler took the food prepared for the Sultan and went to taste it. When he came back a little later, he said, "Take the tray inside."

He would taste all of the Sultan's food first. It was a kind of test for poison. There were many sultans in the past who had been killed by poisoning. When the tray went inside, my excitement increased many times over. I began to wait at the door. I don't know how much time passed, but it seemed like a century to me. *Why am I so excited?* I thought. Again I had begun to pay attention to worldly things. I was growing more and more remote from my dervish training. I wondered what the others at the dervish lodge would think of this state of mine. My hand suddenly went to my sash. I blushed.

I thought of the head butler—the man who ate food that might be poisoned so that the Sultan would not die. This man whom the Sultan entrusted his life to must be very valuable, but at the same time he was the soul whom the Sultan forewent first saying, "You die instead of me!" What kind of paradox was this? There were also head butlers in the past who had betrayed their sultan; they said, "You die instead of me!" Later their heads would be taken first. A difficult job at any rate. Why didn't cooking in the kitchen suffice for a person?

36

The door opened and the head butler came through the door. He said, "The Sultan said that your food remained in the shadow of the plate."

What did this mean? I quickly turned around and began walking straight towards the kitchen. It had remained in the shadow of the plate? In other words, he liked the plate, but he didn't like the food. Wasn't he able to say, "Thank God, I ate another dinner without poison?"

When I returned to the kitchen, Jalabi curiously asked, "What happened, Umar?"

"My food remained in the shadow of the plate," I said.

"What do you mean?"

"What could it mean? The Sultan didn't like my food."

"It's not easy to please the Sultan. This is your first meal; don't worry. You have a lot of time; of course, you will make his food again," said Jalabi.

The butler coming down the stairs left the dishes in the dishwashing room. When the plate with the fish on it was washed, I put it under my apron and started walking towards the small palace. It was dark outside. I was going to go to my room, but I changed my mind and went to the wooden dock on the edge of the lake. And I threw the plate with the fish on it, which had ruined everything, into the lake. Maybe I would be exiled from here because of this plate. Then, how would I see Mahpari again?

My inner voice said, "Umar, you are going to drown in this worldly life." I returned to my room with complete emptiness in my inner world.

Seljuk plate with eagle (13th century)

Mahpari

Her mother gave birth to her after she had lost her father. Her big brother Jalabi was eight years-old when she was born. During the pregnancy, her mother had looked at the lake so much that Mahpari carried the lake in her eyes.

She was happy. Because she never knew her father, she didn't know fatherly love either. Her love came from her brother and mother.

This small town was her whole world. The lake, the opposite shores, and the mountains in the distance—what a big place this was. The three of them had no one but themselves. Their ancestors had come here with the great migration, and everyone had settled in different places. This had become their home since their father had left her, her mother and Jalabi here.

Her mother, Mihri, was a hard-working woman. Formerly, she had worked in the wheat fields; now she worked in the flour mill where she sifted flour with sieves. In this town, only women sifted flour. She left her home in the morning light and returned in the evening darkness; she never complained about this situation. They accepted everything. Their mother read and explained things to them, sent them to teachers and raised them. Jalabi's cooking at the palace was due to her.

Days Pass

I didn't count days very well. For me there was yesterday and the day before that; in other words, one and two. The rest were "days" for me. Days had passed since I came to the palace. My life was quieter, or I had become accustomed to the commotion and it had become to seem like calm to me.

Days had passed when Mahpari was in my dreams, the treatise was under my pillow, and the fish-plate was in the bottom of the lake.

The next day was the first day of Ramadan, and the Sultan was going to pass Ramadan at Kubadabad. For weeks, spices, vegetables, vinegar, oil and honey were being transported from the caravans to the palace. The flour depots of the bakeries were filled up, and everyone was waiting for these sacred days to come.

The first *iftar* (fast-breaking dinner) table would be set up. The Sultan made the first *iftar* with the people and a table seemingly without end would be set up in the courtyard. Food would be eaten plentifully, but the variety would be small. For this was not a banquet. Work had long-since begun in the kitchen. Tomorrow the whole city and palace members would eat the same food. Tomorrow there would be:

Wheat Soup (Buğday Çorbası)

Dates

Pastrami (Kadid/Pastırma)

Liver with Vinegar (Sirkeli Ciğer)

Tirit with Lentils and Sugar (Mercimekli Şekerli Tirit)

Honey and Grape Sherbet (Bal ve Üzüm Şerbeti)

Even though the master chefs didn't allow me to cook much after the Sultan did not like my first dinner, I made up for it later on. This time, Jalabi and I were going to make *tirit*. Not only us, but at least ten more masters were going to make *tirit*. This was a very important dish for us. Stale bread was not thrown away, but was used in this dish. This was the reason it was so widely available in the bazaars. Bread is considered sacred and stale bread is not to be thrown away. For this reason, there would definitely be *tirit* on the table, especially on the first day. Stale bread would be dried for days on copper trays. Very dry bread would absorb more broth and was more delicious. What was important for our tirit was not its being sweet or salty, but there being stale bread on the table.

Because stale bread was always used, bread would begin to be dried ten days ahead of time for the first day of Ramadan. During this month, kitchen work was done more in the evening. The kitchen was not opened in the morning, but after

42

noon had passed. When one was hungry, he did not stay too long in the kitchen. When preparations were completed, we left the kitchen. After eating the evening meal, I went to the mosque to perform the first Tarawih Prayer and to welcome Ramadan. Then I was going to the square to have a look at the entertainments prepared for Ramadan. The real entertainment would start tomorrow night, but this evening would be festive too.

During Ramadan not only the kitchen, but the market was not open during the day either. Opening some time before *iftar*, the markets stay open almost until the morning call-to-prayer. The whole city spends their morning and noon time resting at home. I left the mosque and walked to the market. There were some people I knew there; greeting them, I continued to walk. How much had changed now from the Konya streets, where I walked with my head down, to the markets I walked through giving *salam* (greeting) to others. I still missed the lodge.

I was behind in my reading. I had not read much except a few pages from the treatise I had brought with me. Because my mind wasn't focused on it, I hadn't understood anything.

My life was passing, pressing on the deep scars in my heart.

At night, our courtyard was very festive. Everyone was up during the time for sleeping and awaiting *sahur* (the pre-dawn meal before fasting). Some were playing checkers and others were explaining the lessons from their hodjas to others. I got a few dates from the kitchen. Eating the dates, I returned to my room. I drank a bowl of water and fell asleep.

When I woke up, everyone was sleeping. There was no sound from the palace or the town. Saying the time was right, I took my treatise and went to the wooden dock on the edge of the lake. I was going to read it while I had time before I began my work.

Bath tiles, Kubadabad Palace (13th century)

Sahur

The first *iftar* of Ramadan passed uneventfully. Because it was the busiest time for the kitchen, we would not break our fast immediately, but would wait for the rush to subside. We were not able to eat together. For this reason, we kitchen workers were going to have the first *sahur* together. We carried the food ingredients to the small palace kitchen. This time not us, but the masters, assistants and apprentices were going to make the preparations. Special food would be made for *sahur*. Dough-based foods and rice were eaten plentifully in order to keep the stomach full. Very oily or spicy foods were avoided.

Jalabi was going to be with us at *sahur*, too. Even though he said, "Let's go to the village for the entertainments," no one was interested. Plus Ramadan was not running away; it had just begun.

We had sat down all together on the side of the terrace that faced the lake. Tea had been steeped and everything was ready for friendly conversation. Everyone was telling his own story. Other people, other lives, other heroes—everyone had a unique story. Whereas, at the dervish lodge we all thought we had the same story or no one would talk about where he came from and what he did.

Tea was drunk, chess was played and conversation stopped. Just at that moment master Selim called out, "The table is ready." What a table spread! It had everything:

Fried Sausage (Kızarmış Sımsarmak)
Flat Baked Bread (Bazlamaç)
Sweet Batter (Şekerli Bulamaç)
Various Pastry (Börek)
Ring-Shaped Pastry (Küliçe)
Tart Compote (Mahoş Hoşaf)
Ayran
Rose Sherbet (Gülap Şerbeti)

Formerly I would have said, "Should *sahur* be made with this many different dishes?" Now I recited the basmala and sat down. We would eat similar things at the dervish lodge, but not all at the same time. I liked the bread roll I dipped into *ayran* or the *hoşaf* I ate with *börek* the best. This time they were all on the table at the same time. We ate *sahur* with a good appetite from all these things.

I stood up to send Jalabi off. It was time for the morning call-to-prayer. "What are we going to do on *eid* (religious festival)?" Jalabi asked. When he saw me looking at him in astonishment, he added,

"Why are you surprised? The Sultan will spend the Night of Power and *eid* in Konya; we'll have time off."

The Sultan would see my Sheikh in Konya, but when would I see my Sheikh again? Was it going to be possible for me to see her again? Suddenly my heart was aching. "You can spend *eid* with us," he said.

"That's not possible," I suddenly said.

"Why not, Dervish? Your dervishness has surfaced again. Do you have a mother or father?"

"It's not possible; don't insist, Jalabi."

"For God's sake, why not Dervish? You can spend *eid* with my family."

"Don't insist. Have a good night," I said and sent Jalabi off. The pain in my heart increased. Would I see Mahpari at *eid*? My heart couldn't take this. The same thing happened again and I asked the same question.

Which one was Love?

While burning to see my Sheikh, when Jalabi said to come to his family, this time my heart began to hurt more because I would see Mahpari. But it hurt differently. While my love for my Sheikh made my heart burn, my love for Mahpari was piercing my heart like an arrow.

Every love is a unique love. Thinking about this, I lay down on my bed and picked up the treatise.

Don't think that every love is the same. Love burns, love drowns ... Do not see every love as one. Don't forget that this universe, this sky and these stars, are equal to Love. My silent and calm heart was sleeping.

New Life

❦

The Sultan went to Konya from the palace in the last week of Ramadan. The huge palace was empty. He would return after spending *eid* in Konya. It was said that the Sultan loved this palace very much and that he was a poet because of this palace. I spent a lot of time on the terrace facing the lake. It was said, "You already feel the concern that in winter you will not be able to sleep without seeing the lake."

On the twenty-seventh night of Ramadan, I spent the whole night in worship on the rush mat in my room. I didn't eat or drink anything. If I had been at the dervish lodge, I would have done the same thing. My knees had become blood-red from the marks of the mat. I spent the following nights sleeping on the mat. How quickly I had grown accustomed to the wool mattress; I was angry with myself.

Jalabi and I were going to meet at the mosque on the morning of the holiday. Actually I was very excited. I was going to see Mahpari. If they understood something or knew my thoughts, how would I look Jalabi in the face? While waiting at the mosque door with all these worries on my face, I saw Jalabi's smiling countenance. "*Eid mubarak* (happy *eid*), Brother Dervish," he said. I said to myself, "May God always keep Jalabi smiling;" what a sincere person he was.

"Have a happy *eid*, Brother Jalabi," I replied and we embraced. What was brotherhood like? This question stuck in my throat on this holiday morning.

"After the Prayer we'll have breakfast at our house and then we'll go to the fair in the village," Jalabi said.

"OK, we'll go to the fair. Plus I should get a few gifts so I won't come empty-handed."

"That's not necessary, Dervish."

"Why isn't it necessary? Where else am I going to spend this money? I don't want to carry it around anymore. I told you, we don't carry money."

"We'll see, then," Jalabi said and we left the courtyard and entered the mosque.

After the Prayer we went to Jalabi's house. We were standing in front of it. Again that wooden door. Jalabi pushed the door open and we entered the room we had sat in before. This time the table was ready. On the wooden table there were several pieces of bread, cookies and two bowls of steaming soup with meat in it. There was no one around. Worry took the place of my excitement. Had they understood everything? This was the last thing that I wanted.

Beads of cold sweat had flowed down my back during this moment of apprehension. Then the door opened.

"My mother," said Jalabi.

I immediately got up and bowing, I gave her my *salam*. "*Eid mubarak*. I am very grateful that you opened your table to me," I said.

"May you be in good health and happy *eid* to you, too," she replied. "This is just breakfast food. The real banquet is this evening. God willing, you will come back, won't you?" his mother asked. "God willing," I said.

"Mother, where is Mahpari?" asked Jalabi. "She'll come, my son; she is going to have breakfast at the next-door neighbor's," she said and left the room. I calmed down. We began to eat, but I can't say that I was totally myself. I wanted the first moment of encounter to come and pass. I wasn't very much aware of what I ate. We drank a glass of sherbet and left the house.

A fair had been set up on the bazaar grounds. The market was open. There was action everywhere—children and youth—a festive holiday atmosphere. There was a crowd of children in front of the confectioner's shop. "Let's go in, Jalabi. We'll get some candy for both us and the children," I said.

"Let's go," he said.

The sherbet-maker was selling, from trays, the *kadayıf* (kataifi) he had made for *eid*. "Maybe we should get *kadayıf* instead of candy," I said.

"Whatever you like, Dervish," Jalabi said.

When I turned towards the sweets-seller and asked, "How much?"

Jalabi said, "You've learned this job."

"I've learned, but I'm not very happy about it," I said.

"A tray is five *akçe*s," the shopkeeper said.

"Set one tray aside; we'll get it tonight," I said.

"Yes, sir," replied the sweets-seller. I extended the pouch full of *akçe*s and told the shopkeeper to distribute the rest to the children. Then we left the confectioner's shop.

Everyone was in the streets—acquaintances from the palace, tradesmen, sellers, and families going on visits.

We had gone down to the edge of the lake when Jalabi said, "Let's look at the fish counters." There were oarsmen, those in the boats, and fishermen—this was another festive place. A clown was jumping on two poles that had been set up on the edge of the lake. Those watching were on pins and needles. The clown pretended to be falling now and then and the screams were echoing from the water. At a small counter among the fish stands there was a fisherman who fried and sold the fish he had caught.

When Jalabi saw the stand, he said, "Let's go and look."

"Give me a chance to get hungry," I said. "I can't eat on a full stomach like this, Jalabi."

"You're the one who's full. At any rate, you've become a skeleton," he said.

"Give me two fish sandwiches," he said to the fisherman and handed him some money.

After putting the fish in the skillet between two pieces of bread, he added two large pieces of onion and gave us the fish. Although I had complained a little at first, the fish was delicious. With the fish in our hands, we slowly climbed up towards the palace. On the road we ran into some master chefs and assistant chefs who lived in the village. Everyone was in their own world. When we reached the courtyard, because the head butler was in Konya, we were met by Mustaiddin master, who was left in his place. He not only came to meet us, but he offered us some halva he had made. I had been eating something from the time I got up this morning. If this continued, I would pass Jalabi. I didn't really want to eat, but the halva had just been cooked. The almonds had been browned so well that their aroma tickled a person's desire.

The person kissing the hand of master Mustaiddin stepped to the side and exchanged greetings in turn with the others. Finishing the cooking of the halva last, Uzun Efendi came and the *eid* ceremony was finished. Uzun Efendi had come here from Aleppo; due to his height of more than two meters, everyone called him Uzun Efendi (Tall Sir). The master said that the Sultan was going to return after the holiday, but the day of his return was uncertain. We sat on the terrace. It was almost evening and the sun had descended to the mountains.

Jalabi said, "Let's go."

I replied, "I shouldn't be a guest twice in one day; I'll come later on."

"You can't be serious. Mother Mihri will be angry with both of us. She's been cooking since morning. How can I tell her Umar didn't come?" he asked.

Even though I said, "I'll stop by tomorrow," it didn't do any good.

When he said, "That's not acceptable; we'll go now. Didn't my mother tell you to come? We got *kadayıf* for her sake," I lowered my sails. "That's true. Let's go before the confectioner closes his shop."

Bath tiles, Kubadabad Palace (13th century)

Reunion

We got the dessert and went to the house. Again we were in front of that wooden door. My hand was shaking so much from excitement, that I could have dropped the tray. If Jalabi had asked, "What's going on," I wouldn't have known what to say. We opened the door and entered the house. We were in the same sitting room. The table was ready, but there were now four spoons on the table. Were we going to sit all together at the table? This was not very customary here. Strangers did not eat together with the family. While they counted me as a member of the family, I couldn't get Mahpari out of my dreams.

The door opened and Mother Mihri entered with a tray in her hand. As she entered, she called out: "Mahpari, bring the water and sherbet when you come."

A fine, thin and very soft voice replied, "Yes, mother." This was the first time I heard Mahpari' voice. Her calmness, goodness, compassion and loyalty could all be understood from her voice.

When the dining tray was put in front of us, the banquet menu became obvious:

Pit Roasted Lamb (Biryan)

Eggplant Stew (Patlıcan Kalyesi)

Turnips with Meat (Etli Şalgam)

Sweet Pastry with Walnuts (Nukul)

Rice and Saffron Dessert (Zafiranlı Pirinç Tatlısı)

The dishes were holiday dishes bought from the ceramic-maker. While I was looking at the dishes, the door opened again. Mahpari was at the door with a small tray, on which there were two ceramic pitchers.

I lowered my head towards the table. I wasn't ready to come eye-to-eye and face-to-face yet.

Putting the tray on the edge of the wooden table, she said, "Welcome."

Actually, you are welcome; from the moment I first saw you, your eyelashes have been piercing my heart.

"I'm pleased to be here; happy *eid*," I said.

My voice was shaky and came out very choked. Jalabi was on my left and Mother Mihri was on my right. Mahpari sat directly across from me. As she reached for the glass in front of her, I saw her white silky hand. The thinness of her wrist showed her delicacy. My God! What things I was thinking at the table. While looking at her hands, I began to raise my eyes without knowing it. She was wearing a green velvet dress. Raising my head a little more, I saw her white neck and eyes across from me. When she extended water to me, our eyes met. My breathing stopped and I wanted to immediately leave the room and distance myself from here.

Until Mother Mihri said, "Come on, begin, my son. Why aren't you eating?" I hadn't even touched my spoon. Jalabi continued to spoon his food continuously. You would think he had not eaten anything all day. In order not to spoil the situation, I dipped my spoon from one dish to another.

As he continued to chew his food, this time Jalabi said, "I don't understand how you eat one spoon of dessert and then one spoon of food."

I wasn't even aware of what I was eating. I was only able to say, "We ate a lot today; I guess I'm not hungry yet."

After this meal, which seemed to me to last a century, I hurriedly left the house. Now I didn't even know where I was walking. Not even an attack of malaria had been able to hold me back from my speed this time. It was as if I was unable to breathe.

My breath was Mahpari ...

When I came to myself, I found myself on the edge of the lake in front of the fortress on the island. The place where we met in my dreams—were all these things going to be real one day? Were Mahpari and I going to meet at this fortress?

Seljuk bowl with flowers (13th century)

Seljuk bowl with flowers (13th century)

Former Confusion

The Sultan was going to return to the palace today. In particular, he was returning from a hunt. Preparations were made accordingly. If he had been fortunate in the hunt, what he brought back would be cooked; if he had not been successful, something from the kitchen would be cooked. The sherbet-maker was going to bring *faluze* (starch pudding) for dessert.

Jalabi entered the kitchen. He came to my side and said, "Dervish, you appeared and then disappeared. What's the secret to this?" he said laughing. "Why didn't you appear again?" he continued.

Saying, "I didn't have the energy. I slept and rested," I closed the subject.

"It's obvious that you still haven't recovered," he said as he passed on.

Wondering if I had made him angry, I followed him. "What happened, Jalabi? Are you angry?"

"No, it's not important," he said. It was obvious that he was either angry or offended. He was not aware of what I was going through and he was reacting. Whereas, what difficult days I had lived and how much my spirit had ached. I still didn't know what I was going to do, but this idea had begun to take form in my mind: Mahpari, Mother Mihri and Jalabi had the right to know.

Regardless of the outcome, I should tell them. Plus, death was not at the end of this, but this state was worse than death. I went to Jalabi's side again. "Jalabi, come and let's make *faluze*," I said.

"You make it. I'm going to help the kebab-maker," he said.

"You're going to help the kebab-maker, is that right?" I said.

"Yes," he said and he left me and went to the side of the kebab-maker.

Now I had made things more difficult. On the one hand, I was thinking of telling Jalabi about my interest in Mahpari and, on the other hand, I was making him angry. I thought that first of all, I should restore things with Jalabi, so I went to his side.

"Jalabi, I'm sorry. This *eid* was a little heavy for me being together with your family. That is something I am not accustomed to. Now I know. When a person doesn't know, he doesn't feel pain, Jalabi. After he knows, it hurts," I said.

Actually it was just as I mentioned it. If a person doesn't know love, he doesn't look for it. But if he tastes love, he can't do without it. If he has never known his family, but then takes a spoon of soup with a family at someone else's table, then the situation is hopeless.

People can only imagine what they have seen and known. The rest doesn't even come to mind. Now love was standing in front of me. Once it touched your heart, you could not forego it.

You burned, burned, burned...

When he said, "Nothing is wrong, Dervish. You took it so seriously," I was startled. "Come and let's make some halva," he said and we went to the stove.

56

Just at that moment, the master's voice was heard from the door: "The Sultan has arrived." Immediately after that, the Sultan's men entered the kitchen. The hunt had been very bountiful. Duck, pheasant, various kinds of birds. This time the master called out, "Let the table be set in the courtyard this evening."

All was to be made ready in a short time. The assistant chefs had already begun to pluck the birds' feathers. Some were to be broiled, some to be roasted, and some to be baked in the oven. The catch from the hunt was Sultan Kayqubad's favorite dinner. He liked game from the hunt very much. Because he liked it so much, he would share it with everyone. The kitchen had returned to its former days.

Seljuk bowl (13th century)

Seljuk bowl with flowers (13th century)

Dream

After the nightmares I had seen for days, I went to my room thinking that I would sleep comfortably. I sat on my bed and took the treatise from under my pillow. It was a peaceful moment. I had needed this for a long time. The first sentences I read were:

Love

Is always love.

If you leave, its reflection remains.

If you recognize it, it comes with you.

Love

Is your spirit; that's why you can't leave it.

What a miserable love this is, I thought. I was living it and he was writing it. It was as if he was writing about me. When I stretched out on my bed, I felt both sleepy, and awake and peaceful.

She came.

There was a smile on my face. I was between two lives,
neither in this world nor the next.

She ran towards me over the water and reached out her hand.

"Come to the fortress on the island," she said silently.

Then, stepping on the water, she ran towards the island.
She turned her head around and looked.

How could I not follow her? This was not a dream. The dream I saw her in on the first night we met had become real. Mahpari was calling me to the island.

I got up from bed and began to run fast.

The palace walls, the people in the hall, everything began to become nebulous. As if my life had passed in this corridor, it seemed endless. I saw the stone courtyard, but I could not get out. I wasn't getting any closer as time passed.

I was startled by someone I ran into, and the corridor where I continued to run came to an end. When I left the stone courtyard, I started running towards the wooden dock. Sometimes the sky and ground were upside-down, and I felt like I was running in air.

The trees and birds were all getting out of my way.

When I reached the wooden dock, the end of the road had come. The longest run of my life had occurred on this three-foot wide wooden dock. I saw the mother and father I couldn't remember, and the dervish lodge and my master were all on the wooden dock. I couldn't waste my time with anyone; without even giving *salam*, I continued running.

I had come to the edge of the wooden dock.

I stepped on the water. It was a strange moment. While I and my clothing submerged in the water, my spirit and heart continued to run on the water. Suddenly everything became heavy. Deep waters surrounded me. Now all of me had become the maddening green color of the lake—the green of Mahpari's eyes.

Everything became heavier and heavier. Everyplace had become deep green like the ceramic walls of the palace. This is peace, I thought.

Where was Mahpari?

Where was the island?

Island ...

The green ... of peace.

Konya's green.

The maddening green of the lake ...

The green of Mahpari's eyes ...

The green of my nothingness ...

Green ...

While a piece of paper from my sash that had mixed with the lake's green floated before my eyes.

Seljuk eagle (13th century)

Section II

2010

Bath tiles, Kubadabad Palace (13th century)

The Longest April

The road was very beautiful. Kubadabad Palace which I had excitedly waited for years to see would soon be before my eyes. Actually, that was the main reason I had wanted to attend the conference at Beyşehir. While all this excitement was rippling in my head, two kilometers later I suddenly saw the Beyşehir Lake before my eyes.

In reality, after this, nothing was going to be the same.

For the first time before me was that green of the dishes that I had gathered together in my ceramic collection, the green of peace, the green that left the sultans sleepless, the maddening green, the green that stole my peace and the green that was my peace. I froze, life stopped and I got out of the car. Maybe I should never have seen it.

I would meet Kubadabad Palace on the edge of the lake forty kilometers later. What a road. It was the most unbelievable road I had seen in the thousands of kilometers of travel that I had made so far in Turkey.

Where did this Kubadabad curiosity come from?

I had always been in awe of the Seljuks. This awe increased many fold in every work I saw. Each work was at the summit of intelligence, mathematics, and art. I had not been able to tear myself away from the door of the Ulu Mosque in Divriği for two days. When I first saw the Kubadabad Palace tiles in a book, I tore out the page where the broken plate was and ran to the side of ceramics master Ibrahim. At the end of two months, that plate was now in my home. I gave it a unique place in my whole collection. It would always be like that. This was the beginning of my Kubadabad obsession.

Bath tiles, Kubadabad Palace (13th century)

A Calm Afternoon

Two stones on top of one another were what remained of what they called Kubadabad. The only palace remaining from the Seljuks was in this state. All the tiles had been unjustly taken to Konya, but its spirit which had not been able to be replaced for centuries stood majestically before me. I became engrossed in thought; it was as if I saw it. I shuddered suddenly. How was this possible? I had never seen this place before.

"I am like I was when I first came here 770 some years ago,

I still come to find peace here ever since I lost it here.

Your eyelashes in the palm of my hand in the stone courtyard of Kubadabad

The moon rising above the lake ...

And a silent night ...

The waters have risen, the season is autumn,

your shadow on the stairs descending from the stone courtyard,

Two lost lives, a black dream and your eyelashes burning in my palms."

Without thinking too much, I made the conference and, finishing my work at the school, I settled in the hotel saying I was tired as an excuse. The Beyşehir Lake was spread beneath my feet from my room on the top floor of the hotel. I looked towards the lake and became absorbed in thought. I felt very strange. What were these snow-capped mountains, this month of April, this green, and these streets signs of?

Seljuk plate (13th century)

Past Day and New Day

I started walking around the Beyşehir streets with the hope of running into other things. It was just the time for roving around. I had several hours before the evening meal. I went down to the edge of the lake; the color of the sky and the lake was unbelievable. It was crowded at this hour. I think that this is my favorite time in Anatolian cities. The city was alive.

Walking from the edge of the lake to the German Bridge, I went to the marketplace. Some of the shops were closed and some were about to close. There were lines in front of the bakeries. "Who knows in how many cities I have seen this bustle," I smiled. This was life for me. Not waiting in heavy traffic while going home by car or waiting at a bus stop, but walking along an avenue in the midst of the bakery's aroma and arriving home—this was life, even if no one here was aware of it.

I descended to a square to the right of the avenue; I saw an antique-dealer's shop sign next to a fruit and vegetable market. Its doors were closed. I was surprised when I looked inside the small display window. It was as if the ten square meter shop would collapse on top of me. The place where I would come the next morning before leaving was settled.

Slowly going toward the car, I set out towards the restaurant where we would eat fish from Beyşehir's bountiful lake. I guess I wasn't alone, but I still felt strange.

I looked out from the restaurant's window all night long. The tandoor fish I ate seemed to remind me of the distant past. But I couldn't pin-point what I remembered. How could a fish that I was eating for the first time remind me of something?

Fish Tandoor

Fish from the Beyşehir Lake

Onion

3 tablespoons vinegar

1 tablespoon butter

Salt

Clean the fish and divide into pieces. Put the prepared fish in an oven tray. Add salt, vinegar, oil and large slices of onion. Mix all ingredients, bake in the oven and serve.

On the one hand, I thought about all I had experienced that day; my mind was very tired and I needed a good night's sleep. I returned to the hotel. I immediately fell asleep with the idea that I would stop by at the antique dealer's shop before I set out on the road.

I awoke to a beautiful scene in the morning. I had opened the floor-length hotel curtains the night before. When I opened my eyes, all the green of the lake surrounded me. It was a magnificent moment. I don't know how long I remained looking at the scenery, but now I had to leave. With the discipline gained by years of travel, I was in my car in ten minutes. Now I was going to the small antique-dealer's big shop. Why did I say big? At the evening meal I had learned the place of the essential depots and now I was headed there. I parked in front of the big depot and knocked on the iron door. The person who would meet me knew I was coming and would accompany me on this tour.

There were ten separate depots, each the size of a football field, and they were all full of objects. This could not be true. In the first place I entered there were marble pools and sinks, old wooden kitchen ventilation equipment and Konya earthenware jars on the floor. It was as if all the material from old houses everywhere in Turkey had come here. The marble sinks were unbelievable.

Then we passed to the factory section next to it. You might ask, "What is that?" Old wooden olive presses, equipment for squeezing *tahin* and pounding wheat and much more. All the wooden apparatus of old factories were here. The wooden olive press resembled my grandfather's press in Kilis.

When we entered the depot containing dishes, my excitement increased many fold. Regardless of how much I think I am a traveler, actually I am a chef. And I love nothing better than to make food for old dishes. I saw *kınık* plates here for the first time, and what a collection it was. The simplicity of the colors running over them was so unique that I cannot describe it. Perhaps hours had passed while I was lost among the plates. The two green plates I saw at the side as I was walking out the door were signs of this journey. I could not take my eyes off them. For many eyes they were just two ordinary plates. But for me, their simplicity was their crown. Both their glazes had diminished; green paint had been dripped on top of the green color of one of them. Their simplicity struck me. I asked their price, but then I remembered to look in my pocket. I guessed the plates would remain here for some time more. As for me, I would come to Beyşehir one more time to buy these green plates.

Hey Beyşehir,

I am not leaving you behind, but in my inner peace ...

Bath tiles, Kubadabad Palace (13th century)

Everything Is Upside-down

It was as if I had been in a dream for the last two weeks. I don't know where this journey I had now set out upon again would lead me, but the one thing I did know was that this time I had the money to buy the plates. I hadn't even understood how the trip had passed when I saw the Beyşehir Lake and relaxed. All the questions in my mind were ended and the green peace had found me. I made the plan in my head long ago. I was going to walk the streets of Beyşehir and read about the city. I dropped off my suitcase at the hotel. I was going to immediately go to the school across from the hotel and scan some of the books in the library. This place was so familiar that it was not hard for me to enter. While I was lost among the books, I was startled by the words of the librarian:

"We're closing."

"OK, I'm leaving, but can I take out the books?"

She said it would not be a problem.

While happily leaving there, I remembered that I had promised to eat tandoor fish with my teachers. This time we were going to eat fish at the Yaka Monastery, where we could view Beyşehir from the top. I hadn't been able to go there the last trip due to a lack of time. After dinner, I went to the hotel. I worked a little and then fell asleep watching the moonlight falling on the lake. I woke up early in the morning. I was going to descend to the edge of the lake. Leaving the hotel, I walked for ten minutes on a path that led me to the wooden dock at the edge of the lake. Saying, "What a beautiful morning," "What beautiful water," and "What beautiful snow-capped mountains," I walked towards the end of the dock. Perhaps unknown to myself, I had arrived at a point that would change my life from top to bottom. Bending over, I looked at the water. The water was placid, green and glass-like. Suddenly I saw a reflection in the water. What was the turban doing on my head? The person I saw was not me. Then who was this man looking at me from the water?

Seljuk bowl with flowers (13ᵗʰ century)

Journey

Who was it that I had seen in the water?

I was going to ask myself this question for a long time—who had I seen in the water? While roaming around the streets of Beyşehir with this question in my mind, I decided to go to the antique dealer to buy the plates that had brought me here. I knocked on the door of the depot. When it opened, the smell I sensed the last time caressed my face. I said hello and entered and walked straight to the section where the plates were. Again the plates were before me waiting like a lover awaits her beloved; they were waiting for the moment of union in the same place. While the antique dealer's assistant wrapped the plates, I began walking around the depot. Wooden, glass, and marble objects and large jugs. So many things each with a unique smell and story. Thinking, "A person could spend weeks in this shop," I paid the money and left.

I was going to put these plates next to the Kubadabad plate with the fish on it.

The things I had experienced since I came to Beyşehir had worn me out. It felt like someone was with me while I wandered around the streets. What was the whole city saying? Was it a clue? I needed to calm down a little. As these things came to mind, I wanted to leave.

Beyşehir Again

Now I was beginning every trip in Beyşehir and ending every trip in Beyşehir. This was the third time I had come in the last month. I had become accustomed to being here. In spite of my heavy workload, I couldn't forego this town.

This place had changed me. I had not become completely different, but I had changed. I was sometimes living in a dream. The other night when I saw the nightmare that brought me here again, I got up and went to my study; I wrote the words below at that time of night.

When I got up in the morning, I didn't remember anything, but when I saw this paper on my desk and read the writing on it, I remembered my experience that night. I immediately gathered my things together and set out. The writing was as follows: "I am not going to see anyplace else! This is it..."

I am writing from the sleep I awoke from centuries later.

I am saying it again;

I have sealed my eyes; I am not going to look at any other place.

Now I remember everything;

The centuries-old plate that I saw yesterday at the antique dealer's shop, and which I could not leave behind, was as if my own plate.

A person sometimes finds his soul mate centuries later.

Now I am forgetting everything I know,

This was not me and I am going.

The face I saw when I first looked at my reflection in the maddening green water was not me either; now I remember.

I am setting out on a journey that will last for centuries.

Last year I made a copy from a picture of the plate with a fish on it that had been found among the ruins of Kubadabad. I had always carried that plate in the pupil of my eye. That plate was witness to everything.

I came to Beyşehir again. I had many things on my mind. Walking among the ruins of the palace and taking long walks, I was going to stay here until I found something new.

The only thing I am searching for now is the food he made then.

Yes, I am very curious about what food he made then. Yes, I am an incorrigible chef...

Since the time these thoughts began to circulate in my mind, I have tried to find all the sources I could. Second-hand book dealers, hand-written works, legends, neighboring states in the same centuries and food records, food records in places where the Seljuks came and much, much more. Now I am at the beginning of a longer road and I am very curious as to what food he cooked.

Finding sources again and again, I bring them to my new address, the Beyşehir hotel. The hotel was on a hill just across from the lake. The whole lake was at my feet. Because looking at it might help me remember the past, I pulled my desk to the window. For now my days pass with reading; I will be happier when I start writing.

I don't know how many days passed. I began walking towards the wooden dock where I first saw him while looking at my reflection in the water. Again I sat on the dock.

"What a beautiful morning, what a beautiful sky, and what beautiful snow-capped mountains," I said to myself. The sound of the fishing boat motors disturbed all the morning's calm. The two fishermen in the blue boat passing in front of me were throwing out their nets. Then they stopped the motor and began to gather the nets on the other side. They were putting their hands in the lake and gathering the nets. This moment was very normal for this situation, but it reminded me of something. Although I had come to the lake time and again, I had never touched the water. Yes, yes, I had never touched this lake's water.

I went down the steps on the edge of the dock. There was a broader step there. I stood there and rubbed my hand on the surface of the water. Then I put my hand in deeper and moved it from right to left. Suddenly several unintelligible words fell from my lips;

"The last thing he had touched in Beyşehir was this water."

Now what did this mean? I was confused again. But not giving it much significance, I returned to my books to learn what he had cooked and eaten.

Seljuk plate (13th century)

Seljuk plate (13th century)

Section III

Seljuk Cuisine Recipes

Recipes List

1. SOUPS

2. SNACKS

3. BANQUET DISHES

4. DESSERTS

5. SHERBETS AND DRINKS

- I -

SOUPS

Dry Wheat Soup
(Kuru Buğday Çorbası)

2 pound wheat

3 teaspoons salt

2 pound yogurt

5 cups water

1 teaspoon dry mint

2 tablespoons butter

Crush the wheat in a mortar. Mix the ground wheat with salt and yogurt. Make balls the size of walnuts from the thickened yogurt. Spread these lumps on a clean cloth and flatten them on top. Dry these yogurt-wheat patties for about 10 days. Put 10 patties in a medium pot with water. Lower the heat when the water boils. Heat the mint in the butter in a medium pan and add to the soup. Turn off the heat and serve. Preserve the remaining patties in a cloth bag and use when desired. During the time of the Seljuks, those who made and sold pure clarified oil were called *semman*.

Serves 4 to 6.

Tandoor Soup
(Tandır Çorbası)

½ cup chickpeas

½ cup beans

½ cup green lentils

3 cups meat broth

½ cup bulgur

1 teaspoon salt

5 cups water

1 medium onion

2 tablespoons braised meat

Soak chickpeas, beans and green lentils overnight. Put broth, soaked pulses, bulgur, salt and water in a large pan on stove and turn on heat. When the water begins to boil, add finely chopped onion and meat. Cook over low heat for approximately 1 hour and serve.

Serves 8.

Lamb Noodle Soup
(Tutmaç Çorbası)

For the soup:

1 pound finely ground lamb

6 cups water

1 teaspoon salt

2 pound strained yogurt

3 garlic cloves

4 tablespoons butter

For the dough:

2 cup flour

1¼ cups water

½ small bowl of butter

Put meat and water on stove. While meat is cooking, knead the dough with flour and water. Allow the dough to rest for half an hour. Roll out the dough with the help of an *oklava* (long, thin rolling pin). Cut the dough you have opened into small squares (⅓ inch x ⅓ inch), sprinkle flour on them and allow to rest. After cooking the meat approximately 1½ hours, add the pieces of cut dough and salt to the pot and lower the heat. Begin to beat the yogurt with l cup of water in a mixing bowl. Crush the garlic and add to yogurt. Continue to beat the yogurt, adding soup broth little-by-little with the help of a ladle. When the yogurt becomes warm, add it to the slowing cooking soup. After this, when the soup begins to boil again, turn off the heat. As a final step, brown the butter in a small pan, add it to the soup, and serve. There is a record to the effect that when Sultan Tughril Bey of the Great Seljuk State took several bites of the food he was served when he took Nishapur, he said, "The *tutmaç* is good, but it has no salt and garlic."

Serves 8.

Liver Soup
(Ciğer Çorbası)

½ pound lamb liver

1 medium onion

2 tablespoons butter

1 tablespoon flour

4 tablespoons vinegar

1 teaspoon salt

5 cups water

2 tablespoons minced parsley

Boil the lamb liver as a whole in a medium pot full of water for 10 minutes. Then drain the lamb liver, put it on a cutting board, and cut the liver into tiny pieces. Dice the onion. Put the lamb liver and onion in a medium pot and begin to brown them slowly in butter. Putting flour on the mixture, continue browning. Add the vinegar, salt, and 5 cups of water to the pot and cook for 20 minutes more. Turn off the heat and sprinkle parsley on top of the soup. Put the lid on the pot, allow to rest 5 minutes and serve. In the time of the Seljuks, those who made vinegar were called *sirka-furush*.

Serves 4 to 6.

Noodles with Salted Yogurt
(Tuzlu Yoğurtlu Şehriye)

5 cups water

2 cups home-made noodles

1 pound salted yogurt

2 tablespoons dry mint

3 tablespoons butter

Put the water in a medium pot and bring it to a boil. Add noodles and boil for 10 minutes. While the noodles are boiling, add salted yogurt, spoon by spoon. Boil together for 10 minutes more. Heat mint in butter in a small pan and serve soup. Salt is not needed because salted yogurt is used. After yogurt is strained, it is salted and pressed into earthen jugs. It was preserved to use at meals and breakfast. A simple dough of flour, water and salt would be rolled out. This dough would be cut into thin strips and made into noodles. The noodles would be dried and stored in cloth bags and used as needed.

Serves 4 to 6.

Wheat Soup

(Buğday Çorbası)

1 cup wheat

1 teaspoon salt

6 cups water

1 cup yogurt

4 tablespoons butter or olive oil

1 tablespoon dried mint

Crush the wheat in a mortar. Put the crushed wheat in a medium pot and add salt and water. Cook for approximately 45 minutes until wheat is cooked. When the wheat is almost done, beat the yogurt in a mixing bowl and add several ladles of boiling water to it. Slowly add the yogurt to the boiling soup. When it boils again, turn the stove burner off. Heat the butter in a pan and add the mint. Pour the mint-butter on the soup and serve.

Serves 4 to 6.

- II -
SNACKS

Barley Bread

(Arpa Ekmeği)

For the yeast:

1 cup barley flour

5 cups 50 degree water

For the bread:

2 cups barley flour

1 teaspoon salt

Water as needed

First mix 1 cup barley flour and hot water in a deep bowl. The dough should be batter-consistency. When the dough becomes sticky, cover it and allow to rest overnight. The next day add 2 cups barley flour to the dough. Add salt and as much water as is needed and begin to knead. When the dough becomes smooth, divide it into 10 pieces. Flatten the pieces of dough in your hand. Open a walnut-sized hole in the middle of the pieces. Bake the pieces of dough in a tandoor or oven at 170ºC (338ºF) for 30 minutes.

During the time of the Seljuks, millers were called *asiyaban*.

Serves 8 to 10.

Rice with Pepper
(Biberli Pilav)

2 cups rice

2 cups water

4 tablespoons butter

1 teaspoon salt

1 teaspoon black pepper

Wash the rice well. Allow rice to stand in hot water for ½ hour. Put half the butter in a wide pan and brown the drained rice for 5 minutes. Add 2 cups of water to the rice. Add the salt and reduce heat to low. When the rice has absorbed the water, turn off the heat. Sprinkle black pepper on top of the rice. Brown remaining butter in a skillet. Pour browned butter on top of rice and close the cover again. Allow to steep for 10 minutes and serve.

During the time of the Seljuks, rice-sellers were called *birinc-furush*.

Serves 4 to 6.

Pickled Turnips

(Şalgam Turşusu)

2 pound turnips

5 cups water

1 cup vinegar

1 teaspoon mustard

3 tablespoons salt

2 garlic cloves

Wash the turnips and slice into rings. Put turnips and water in a large pan and bring to a boil. Turn off the heat and allow to stand for 1 hour. Add the vinegar, salt, mustard and garlic to the warm water. Ladle them into a glass jar and close the cover. Serve 15 days later.

Serves 10.

Wild Plants with Yogurt
(Borani)

2 pound wild plants
(mallow, labada (Rumex), sorrel)

1 medium onion

⅓ cup olive oil

1 teaspoon salt

3 garlic cloves

½ pound yogurt

Wash the wild plants well. Boil them for 5 minutes in a large pot full of water and drain. Begin to brown the diced onion in a skillet in olive oil. Add the wild plants to the browning onion and stir together. Add the salt, cook 10 minutes more and remove from heat. Add crushed garlic to yogurt, pour on top of borani and serve.

During the time of the Seljuks, workers in gardens and orchards were called *baghban*. Farmers were called names like *barzgar*, *ahl az-zar*, *al-zurra*, *muzari'a*, and *fallah*

Serves 4 to 6.

Eggplant with Vinegar
(Sirkeli Patlıcan)

2 pound eggplant

4 tablespoons vinegar

1 teaspoon salt

¼ cup olive oil

Begin to roast the eggplants in a coal fire (or in an oven at 200ºC (392ºF)). While the eggplants are roasting, mix together the vinegar, salt and olive oil in a bowl. Peel the roasted eggplants and crush on a wooden cutting board. Put the crushed eggplants on a service plate. Pour the oil with vinegar on top and serve.

Serves 4 to 6.

Flatbread
(Girde Ekmeği)

7 cups flour
1 teaspoon salt
4 cups water

Mix flour and salt. Open a hole in the middle of the flour and, slowly adding water, begin to knead. When it becomes dough, cover with a damp cloth and after standing 10 minutes, knead again. Repeat 3 times. Divide the dough into balls the size of your fist. Roll out the balls on a wooden surface with a rolling pin. Be careful that the thickness of the balls is 3 mm and that they are round. Bake the sheets of dough on an iron plate grill or in a *tandoor*.

Four words are found in Seljuk records for iron plates for cooking or *tandoor*: *habbaz*, *nanba*, *nan-paz*, and *nan-wa*.

Serves 8.

Spinach and Bulgur with Yogurt

(Ispanaklı Bulgurlu Borani)

2 pound spinach

1 medium onion

⅓ cup olive oil

1 teaspoon salt

⅓ cup bulgur

⅓ cup water

3 garlic cloves

½ pound yogurt

Wash the spinach well. Chop the washed spinach into few pieces. Begin to sauté the chopped onion with olive oil in a large pot. When the onion is sautéed, add the spinach and sauté together. When the spinach has wilted, add salt, bulgur, and water. Stir the ingredients together and close the lid. Simmer for 20 minutes. Combine garlic with yogurt and serve with *borani*.

Serves 4 to 6.

Lentil Dish

(Mercimek Yemeği)

1 pound red lentils

6 cups water

2 teaspoons salt

2 medium onions

⅓ cup olive oil

5 garlic cloves

Wash lentils well and put in a medium pot. Cover with water and turn on heat. When the lentils begin to boil, remove the foam. Add salt and simmer. Meanwhile, finely chop onions. Sauté the onion in olive oil. Crush 5 garlic cloves in a mortar. When the lentils become mushy, add the garlic and onion and turn off heat. Put the lid on the pot and allow to stand 5 minutes before serving.

Serves 4 to 6.

Flat Baked Bread

(Bazlamaç)

5 cups flour

½ cup hot water

1 teaspoon salt

2½ cups water

Put 1 cup of flour in a bowl. Pour ½ cup hot water on flour and mix. Allow the mixture to stand overnight in the kitchen. The next morning, begin to knead the dough, 2½ cup water, salt, and remaining flour together. When the dough becomes soft, divide it into pieces. With the help of a rolling pin, roll out ⅓ inch thick, 7 inch circles. Cook the circles on an iron sheet grill, in a tandoor, or in a large pan, and serve.

There was another kind of bread made with 3 cups of water during the time of the Seljuks. A piece of dough made from salt dough would be left for the next morning and then made again and again. Flatbreads with cheese, ground beef and wild plants were probably cooked on an iron sheet grill or in the *tandoor*.

Serves 8.

Börek Pastry with Spinach
(Börek)

For dough:

4 cups flour

1 teaspoon salt

2 ½ cups water

1 teaspoon butter

For filling:

1 pound spinach

2 medium onions

4 tablespoons braised lamb

2 tablespoons butter

1 teaspoon salt

½ teaspoon black pepper

Mix flour and salt on a clean board. Open a hole in the middle of the flour mixture and begin to slowly add water. When the water is sufficient, knead hard. Divide into 5 balls when the dough is ready. Cover balls with a clean damp cloth and allow to stand. Wash spinach well and chop. Chop onion. Put the braised lamb, butter, and onion in a large pan. Sauté the meat with the onion for 15 minutes and then add spinach, salt, and black pepper. Sauté all ingredients 10 minutes more until the spinach is wilted and turn off heat. Spread this filling in another bowl and allow to cool. Meanwhile, roll out the balls of dough to the size of a large circle (10 inches) with the help of a rolling pin. Spread the filling in the middle of a circle and close like an envelope. Heat the iron plate grill or a large pan and oil it with butter. Spread butter on the front and back of the *börek* occasionally and cook. Serve the cooked *börek* while hot.

There are records to the effect that *börek* and their varieties were eaten during the time of the Seljuks. Although I just give one recipe here, it is also possible to find ground beef, gristle, cheese, sweet, and wild plant *börek*s. We know that they were usually made on iron plate grills or *tandoor* ovens.

Serves 5.

Ring-Shaped Pastry
(Küliçe)

For yeast:

1 cup barley flour

1 cup water (50 degrees hot)

For dough:

2 cups wheat flour

1 tablespoon butter

1 teaspoon salt

1 cup water

Mix barley flour and hot water in a deep bowl and cover. Allow the dough to stand overnight. The next day add wheat flour, butter, and salt to the dough and begin to knead. Slowly add water as needed. When the dough is ready, break off small pieces of dough (medium apple-sized) and round them with your hands. When they have become 10 inch strips, wet both ends and stick together. Bake the pastries in a tandoor or oven at 180°C (356°F) for 25 minutes. Serve hot.

Serves 6 to 8.

Opo Squash Stew
(Su Kabağı Kalyesi)

2 medium onions

2 pouns opo squash

Water as needed

1 cup boiled chickpeas

1 teaspoon salt

1 teaspoon black pepper

4 tablespoons unripe grape juice

¼ pound butter

2 tablespoons dried mint

Chop the onions and sauté them in a large pot for a few minutes. Cut the squash into cubes and add them into the pot. Add enough water to cover the squash. When the water begins to boil, add the chickpeas, salt, and black pepper. Cook the squash approximately 30 minutes until it is soft. Before turning off the heat, add the juice of unripe grapes and then turn off heat. Brown butter in another skillet and add mint. Without burning the mint, pour the butter over the squash.
Cover, allow to stand 10 minutes, and serve.

Serves 4 to 6.

Pastrami

(Pastırma)

2 pound livestock meat

2 teaspoons salt

For the coating:

1 tablespoon dry red fenugreek

2 teaspoons red pepper

2 teaspoons salt

2 teaspoons red cumin

Water as needed

Salt the meat and hang in cooler. In order for the meat to become cured, there must be a difference between the day and nighttime temperatures and there must be frost at night. Allow the meat to stand 10 days. After 10 days, wash the meat and press it between two heavy rocks. Keep it in the press for 3 days. Hang the meat in the cooler again to dry. Dry for another 10 days. Prepare a dough from all the ingredients for the coating. Rub the coating all over the pastrami that has dried another 10 days. Again leave to dry. Dry for 6 more days and serve.

There are records to the effect that in the time of the Seljuks, as a simple method of curing meat, a piece of meat would be hung on a tree to dry.

Serves 10.

Sausage

(Sımsarmak)

2 pound liver

2 pound fatty lamb

1 pound tail fat

20 garlic cloves

1 teaspoon salt

1 teaspoon cinnamon

1 teaspoon black pepper

1 teaspoon dry mustard

Sausage skin (lamb intestine) as needed

First chop the liver. Then chop the lamb and tail fat together. Mix the meats. Crush 20 garlic cloves with salt in a mortar. Add the garlic and spices to the prepared meat. Knead well. Fill the skins with the help of a funnel. Dry for 1 week in a cooler; then fry with or without oil in a medium pan.

Butchers were called *kassap* or *sallah* in the time of the Seljuks.

Serves 6 to 8.

Liver with Vinegar
(Sirkeli Ciğer)

2 pound liver

½ pound tail fat

8 tablespoons vinegar

1 teaspoon mustard

½ teaspoon cinnamon

1 teaspoon black pepper

2 teaspoons salt

Flatbread and onion as needed

Chop the liver and tail fat with a large knife. Put fat in a large pot and begin to melt it. When the fat begins to melt, add the liver. Sauté until its juice is absorbed. Add vinegar, mustard and other spices. Stirring all ingredients together, sauté 20 minutes more. Serve with flatbread and onions.

Serves 6 to 8.

Tirit with Lentils and Sugar

(Mercimekli Şekerli Tirit)

2 cups green lentils

5 cups water

8 slices of stale bread

1 cup sugar

1 teaspoon cinnamon

Boil lentils in water for 25 minutes; drain to release the dark color. Cover the lentils with water again and leave to boil. Cut up stale bread and put it into bowls. Divide the boiled lentils and sugar among the bowls on top of the bread. Sprinkle with cinnamon and serve.

Ibn Battuta noted that this dish was especially eaten on *eid* (religious festivals).

Serves 6 to 8.

Batter

(Bulamaç)

2 cups flour

⅓ pound butter

1 cup sugar

Begin to brown the flour in butter in a medium pan. When its color begins to turn brown, add the sugar. When the sugar melts in it, serve. It can be eaten by dipping bread into it.

Serves 4 to 6.

- III -
BANQUET
DISHES

Chickpea Stew
(Nohutlu Yahni)

2 cups chickpeas

4 tablespoons butter

2 pound cubed lamb

2 medium onions

2 teaspoons salt

½ teaspoon black pepper

8 cups water

Allow the chickpeas to stand in water overnight. Drain them in the morning. Put the butter in a large pot and turn on the heat. When the butter is browned, add the lamb and diced onion. Add salt and black pepper to the sautéed ingredients. Continue to stir and sauté the meat for approximately 15 minutes. Add the water and chickpeas and turn the heat down low. Cook for approximately 1½ hours and serve.

In Seljuk cuisine stew is not only made from chickpeas; it was also made with parsley, chicken, garlic, and cumin.

Serves 8 to 10.

Fish Tandoor

(Balık Tandır)

3 pound Beyşehir Lake fish
or any other fresh-water fish

2 teaspoons salt

4 tablespoons vinegar

3 tablespoons butter

2 medium onions

Clean and divide the fish into pieces. Put the prepared fish on a tray. Add salt, vinegar, butter, and thick onion slices. Mix all ingredients, bake at 180ºC (356ºF) in the oven for 30 minutes and serve.

Serves 4.

Roasted Kebab with Eggplant
(Patlıcanlı Çömlek Kebabı)

½ pound tail fat

1 pound cubed lamb

2 medium onions

2 pound eggplant

2 teaspoons salt

15 garlic cloves

10 sour plums

1 cup water

Chop fat with a large knife. Put the fat and meat together in an earthen pot or a large pot and begin to sauté over low heat. Continue to sauté for approximately half an hour. While meat is cooking, chop onions into large pieces. Peel eggplants in stripes, cut into large pieces, rub with salt and wash. Then add onions and sauté together. Add whole garlic cloves, eggplant, and plums. After adding salt and water, close the lid of the pot. Simmer over low heat for 1 hour. Let stand for 10 minutes and serve.

Serves 6 to 8.

Meat Paste

(Herise)

1 pound dry wheat

1 pound cubed lamb or chicken meat

8 cups water

2 teaspoons salt

½ pound butter

2 teaspoons cumin

Allow wheat to stand in water over night. Put the cubed lamb with water and salt in a large pot on the stove. After it has cooked for 1½ hours, add the drained wheat. Simmer for 1 more hour. Be careful that it becomes soft and mushy. Add more water if necessary. When it begins to absorb all the water, begin to beat it with a wooden spoon or pestle. The spoon should be made from hornbeam or orange tree wood. Continue beating for approximately 1 hour. When the *herise* forms into strands, remove from heat and pour into service plate. Open a hole in the middle of the *herise*.

Pour butter you have browned into the middle, add cumin, and serve.

A person making *herise* during the time of the Seljuks was called a *harra*s.

Serves 8.

Rice with Meat, Carrots and Chestnuts
(Hasseten Lokma)

4 cups rice

2 pound carrots

1 medium onion

6 tablespoons butter

2 pound cubed lamb

1 cup peeled chestnuts

2 cups boiled chickpeas

4 cups water or broth

2 teaspoons salt

1 teaspoon black pepper

Wash rice well. Allow rice to stand for 1 hour in hot water, in a deep bowl. While waiting for the rice, peel carrots and chop into sticks. Chop onion. Put half the butter into a large pot and begin to sauté the meat. Continue to sauté the meat over a low heat for approximately 45 minutes. Add the chopped carrots, onion and peeled chestnuts to the meat and continue to sauté together. After 15 minutes, when the carrots begin to soften, add the drained rice and boiled chickpeas and sauté 5 minutes more. Add water (or broth) and salt. Turn down the heat very low and put lid on pot. Turn the heat off 20 minutes later, and browning the remaining butter in a skillet, pour on top of rice. Allow to stand for 10 minutes and serve with black pepper.

Serves 8 to 10.

Pit Roasted Lamb
(Biryan)

❦

1 lamb
Bread
Salt
Wood fire
Copper basin

In order to make the baked lamb, dig an outdoors well 1.5 meters deep. Make a wood fire in the well. Wait for the fire to become embers. Put a copper basin full of water on the embers. Put a long, thick stick from one edge of the well to the other. Hanging the lamb which has been divided into two pieces from this stick, lower it into the well. Close the top of the well and wait for about 3 hours for the meat to cook. In addition to the water in the well preventing the fat from dripping on the embers and becoming smoke, it will also prevent the meat from drying. Take the meat out of the well 3 hours later and serve it with salt and bread.

During the time of the Seljuks, makers of *biryan* were called *biryangar* according to records from that time.

Serves 12.

Bread Soaked in Gravy
(Tirit)

7 cups water

5 bones or trotters

2 teaspoons salt

1 teaspoon black pepper

8 slices stale flatbread

5 garlic cloves

1 pound strained yogurt

15 leaves fresh mint

Put the water, bones (or trotters), salt, and pepper into a large pot. Turn heat to medium high and boil for approximately 2 hours. Break the bread into pieces in the bowls. Crush garlic and mix with strained yogurt in a mixing bowl. Pour the boiled broth over the bread. Pour the yogurt with garlic on top. Serve with mint leaves.

We know that the Seljuks liked this dish very much. With a changed recipe, it is still made and liked a lot in Konya.

Serves 8.

Roasted Lamb
(Ateşte Kuzu)

Wood fire

1 lamb

Salt

Light a wood fire outdoors. Rub the lamb meat well with salt. Make an arrangement for the meat to be hung over the fire. The meat should be at least a half meter away from the flames. Place the meat on a wooden pole and hang it over the fire. Turning the meat occasionally, cook it for approximately 3 hours. Put the cooked lamb on a tray and serve.

Serves 12.

Roasted Chicken
(Söğülme Tavuk)

1 whole chicken

1 teaspoon salt

½ teaspoon black pepper

½ teaspoon cinnamon

3 tablespoons butter

Rub the chicken with salt, black pepper, and cinnamon. Oil a copper tray with butter well. Putting the chicken on the tray, put it in the tandoor or oven. Cook at 160°C (320°F) for 1 hour. Serve with flatbread.

This dish can also be made from duck, game, and turkey. There are records to the effect that the Seljuks especially liked game meat.

Serves 4.

Rice with Braised Lamb
(Kalye-i Birinci)

2 pound cubed lamb leg

½ pound lamb tail fat

2 teaspoons salt

4 cups rice

2 tablespoons butter

6 cups water

1 teaspoon black pepper

Clean the nerves from the leg of lamb and cut meat into cubes. Divide the tail fat into small pieces. First melt the fat in a skillet. When the fat begins to melt, add the lamb. Begin to stir and sauté meat. Continue to cook over low heat for 1 hour. When it is almost cooked, add 1 teaspoon salt. Meanwhile, wash the rice well and drain. Begin to sauté the rice with 1 tablespoon butter in a pot. After sautéing for 5 minutes, add water and 1 teaspoon salt. When the water begins to boil, lower the heat. When the rice has absorbed the water, turn off heat and allow to stand for 15 minutes. Brown the rest of the butter in a small pan and pour over rice.

When the rice is ready, serve it with the meat.

Serves 8 to 10.

Partridge or Quail on Skewers
(Şişte Keklik ya da Bıldırcın)

4 partridges or quails

4 skewers

1 tablespoon butter

1 teaspoon salt

½ teaspoon black pepper

After plucking the feathers well, clean the insides of the birds. Rub the prepared birds with butter, salt and black pepper. Put the birds on skewers. Put the skewers over the fire once the wood has turned to embers. Roast 45 minutes, turning, or you may fry them in a pan for 30 minutes, and serve.

There are recipes for this dish from the Seljuks for using wild birds like woodcocks and great bustard.

Serves 4.

Sheep's Head
(Kelle)

1 cleaned sheep's head

Water as needed

1 garlic clove

2 teaspoons salt

5 tablespoons vinegar

1 teaspoons black pepper

Light a wood fire outdoors. Put the head in a cauldron and cover with water. Leave it on the fire all night. In the morning remove the head and shred the meat. Put the shredded meat back into the water on the fire. Crush garlic with salt in a mortar. Add the garlic, vinegar and black pepper to the meat and serve.

A person making sheep's head was called a *rawwas* during the time of the Seljuks.

Serves 8 to 10.

Chicken Kebab
(Tavuk Kebabı)

1 plucked chicken
6 tablespoons vinegar
1 teaspoon black pepper
1 teaspoon salt

Cut the chicken into pieces with a knife. Put the chicken in a deep bowl and rub it with vinegar, black pepper, and salt, and allow to stand 1 hour. Light a charcoal fire. When the charcoal has become embers, throw the chicken pieces into the fire and cook. Serve hot.

People who made kebab during the time of the Seljuks were called *shawwa*.

Serves 4.

Trotters

(Paça)

10 trotters

Water as needed

5 garlic cloves

2 teaspoons salt

10 tablespoons vinegar

Put the trotters in a large pot and cover with water. Light a wood fire outdoors at night and cook the trotters over the fire until morning. In the morning, crush the garlic with salt in a mortar. Add vinegar and stir with a spoon. Add this sauce to the trotters and serve.

We know that the Seljuks liked trotters a lot. They would cook the trotters with a lot of water and then, breaking bread into the broth, they would make *tirit*. A person making trotters was called a *rawwas* by the Seljuks.

Serves 8 to 10.

Brain

(Beyin)

Boiled head

1 teaspoon black pepper

1 lemon, juice extracted

1 teaspoon salt

Split the boiled head with a hatchet after it has cooled. Take out the brain and put it on a service plate. Sprinkle black pepper on it. Serve with lemon and salt.

The brain was the best part of the animal for the Seljuks, and it would be served to important guests.

Serves 4.

Lamb on Skewers
(Sih-i Kebap)

2 pound cubed lamb

1 teaspoon salt

5 tablespoons vinegar

½ pound cubed lamb tail fat

Charcoal fire

4 flat bread

2 medium onions

Rub the meat with salt and vinegar. Skew the meat together with tail fat. Light a charcoal fire and wait for it to become ambers. When the fire dies down, put the skewers on it. While the kebab is cooking, finely chop the onions. Serve the cooked kebabs with flat bread and onions.

A skewer was called a "*sih'i*" by the Seljuks. In addition to the *sih'i*, there was also a skewer called the *bab-zan*. I think that these skewers were served flat and square skewers are used today.

Serves 4.

Buttered Duck
(Yağlı Ördek)

1 duck

1 teaspoon salt

2 teaspoons butter

Rub the duck with salt. Grill it over a wood fire. Occasionally spread butter on the meat while it is cooking.

Another recipe is: Roast the duck in a skillet. Or after rubbing it with salt, cook the duck in a warm *tandoor*. Plain duck was not consumed very much in the time of the Seljuks. It should be served with bulgur, yarma (coarse ground wheat), or rice and flatbread.

Serves 4.

Partridge with Cumin
(Kimyonlu Keklik)

4 plucked pheasants

1 teaspoon salt

1 cup olive oil

1 teaspoon cumin

4 flat bread

Rub the pheasants with salt. Put the olive oil in a copper skillet and begin to heat. Without burning the oil, fry the pheasants on both sides. Sprinkle cumin on top. When the pheasants are fried, serve in the skillet. When the oil has cooled down, dip the flatbread in it and serve.

Serves 4.

Liver Kebab
(Ciğer Kebabı)

2 pound lamb liver

½ pound lamb tail fat

2 teaspoons salt

4 flatbreads

2 medium onions

Light a charcoal fire and cube the liver and tail fat until the fire dies down. Mix the liver and fat on skewers. After salting the meat, put the skewers over the fire and turn until cooked. While the kebab is cooking on the grill, cut the onion very finely. Serve the cooked kebab with flatbread and onions.

Serves 4 to 6.

Stew

(Kalye)

2 pound lamb liver
½ pound lamb tail fat
2 medium onions
2 teaspoons salt
1 teaspoon cinnamon
1 bunch minced parsley
8 flatbreads

Finely chop the liver and tail fat. Chop the onions. Put the tail fat in a large pan and turn on the heat. When the tail fat has melted and browned, add the onion and liver. Add the salt and cinnamon. After sautéing for a half an hour, add the chopped parsley. Serve with flatbread.

Serves 6 to 8.

Eggplant Stew
(Patlıcan Kalyesi)

2 tablespoons butter

1 pound cubed lamb

1 medium onion

5 medium eggplants

5 cups water

2 teaspoons salt

1 pound boiled chickpeas

¼ cup sour grape juice

Put the butter in a large pot and begin to sauté the meat. Chop the onion and add to the meat. Cut the eggplant into strips. Salt and rinse the eggplant. Add the eggplants to the sautéing ingredients. Add water, salt, and chickpeas. Simmer for approximately 1 hour. When the dish is almost done, add the sour grape juice and turn off heat. Allow to stand for 10 minutes and serve.

The Seljuks made stew with all vegetables. This heritage continued in Ottoman cuisine and later in traditional Turkish cuisine.

Serves 4 to 6.

Oven Kebab
(Fırın Kebabı)

1 kid goat

3 teaspoons salt

Copper basin

1 pound butter

10 flatbreads

3 medium onions

Rub the goat with salt. Put it in a copper basin. Put small pieces of butter around it. Put it in a cool oven in the evening. The next morning remove it from the oven and separate the meat from the bones. Serve with buttered bread and onions.

The Seljuks made similar dishes steamed in the oven.

Serves 12.

Turnips with Meat
(Etli Şalgam)

1 pound cubed lamb

2 tablespoons butter

2 medium onions

1 pound turnips

2 cups water

½ cup rice

1 teaspoon black pepper

1 teaspoon cinnamon

2 teaspoons salt

Begin to sauté the lamb in butter over low heat. Add chopped onion to the meat. Meanwhile peel the turnips and wash well. Cut the turnips into cubes and add to the sautéing meat. Sauté for 5 minutes. Add water and allow to boil. When it begins to boil, turn down heat and simmer for a half an hour. Add rice, black pepper, cinnamon, and salt, and continue cooking until rice is cooked. Turn off heat when rice is cooked and serve.

Serves 4 to 6.

Neck

(Gerdaniye)

2 lamb necks

8 cups water

1 teaspoon cinnamon

1 teaspoon salt

Wash the necks well with water. Cook over wood fire outdoors at night. The next morning, add the cinnamon and salt and serve.

It is known that *tirit* is made from the neck broth.

Serves 6 to 8.

Fried Fish

(Balık Tavası)

2 pound Beyşehir Lake fish
or any other fresh-water fish

2 teaspoons salt

1 cup flour

Oil for frying

Clean fish and divide into pieces, and add salt.
Fry the fish you have floured in hot oil.

Serves 6.

Bath tiles, Kubadabad Palace (13th century)

- IV -
DESSERTS

Honey Halva
(Bal Helvası)

½ pound flour
½ pound butter
½ pound honey

Put the flour and butter in a large pan. Begin to brown over low heat. Continue browning for approximately 45 minutes without the flour becoming very dark. When the smell of the flour has gone and it has taken on a gold color, add the honey slowly. Turn the fire off after adding the honey. Serve after cooling for 15 minutes.

A person who made halva was called a *halva-gar* during the time of the Seljuks.

Serves 4 to 6.

Corn Starch Halva
(Nişasta Helvası)

1½ cups of corn starch

4 cups water

⅓ pound butter

3 cups sugar or honey

Mix the corn starch and water in a deep mixing bowl. Put a medium pan on the stove and using a strainer, pour the corn starch water into the pan. When it begins to warm, add butter and sugar (or honey). When the water begins to boil, start to stir it. Stirring constantly for 10 minutes, bring it to the desired consistency. Turn off heat and allow to steep. Serve warm or cold.

Serves 6 to 8.

Halva with Pine Nuts
(Fıstıklı Helva)

3 cups sugar

1½ cups water

½ teaspoon powdered essence of lemon

1 cup pine nutsy

Put the sugar and water in a deep pot, on the stove. When the water begins to boil, add the powdered essence of lemon. Turn off heat when its consistency becomes like a heavy syrup (approximately after 10 minutes). Add nuts. Spread the halva on a marble counter. Divide into small pieces before it gets too cold. Serve after it cools.

Serves 6 to 8.

Akide Candy
(Akide Şekeri)

½ pound water

2 pound sugar

½ teaspoon powdered essence of lemon

⅓ cup water

½ cup sesame

Put water and sugar in pot and bring it to a boil. When the water begins to boil, add the powdered essence of lemon. When the sugar begins to form a paste, add 1 tea glass of water to its center. Continue boiling without stirring. Thus, the sugar will become coagulated. When it attains the right consistency, break off a piece as big as a teaspoon and put it in cold water. If the sugar hardens and breaks, it is the right consistency. Add the sesame seeds, turn off the heat and pour onto a marble counter. When it has cooled enough to touch, begin to roll it and make it into a wick-like strip. Divide into small pieces. When it has cooled and hardened, the *akide* candy is ready. When making this candy, it is necessary for the cauldron to be copper and to have a round bottom.

The Seljuks called candy-makers *shakar-riz*.

Serves 6 to 8.

Flour Halva

(Un Helvası)

2 tablespoons butter

1 cup flour

For sherbet:

2 cups warm water

1 cup grape molasses or honey

Put butter in a large pan. Add flour and begin to brown slowly over low heat. Continue stirring for approximately 1 hour without burning flour. Meanwhile, mix water and grape molasses or honey for the sherbet. When the flour is thoroughly browned, slowly add the sherbet. Stir constantly so the halva does not get lumps. When it becomes completely smooth, turn off heat. Serve hot or cold.

Serves 6 to 8.

Memnuniye Halva

(Memnuniye)

½ pound butter

2 cups semolina

For sherbet:

1 cup grape molasses or honey

2 cups water

Put butter in a deep pan and turn on heat. Add semolina to butter and slowly stir. Continue stirring over low heat for approximately a half an hour. While the semolina is browning, prepare the sherbet by mixing the grape molasses or honey with water in a bowl. When the semolina is golden brown, add the sherbet. Cook for 10 minutes more and turn off heat. Put the lid on the pot and allow halva to steep for 20 minutes; then serve.

Serves 6 to 8.

Nebet Candy
(Nebet Şekeri)

Nebet candy cauldron

Cotton string

Plaster

Sugar

Water

A cauldron for *nebet* candy has holes in its sides and cotton string is strung between these holes. Close the holes with plaster where the strings have been strung so that the candy does not seep out. Boil the sugar and water in another pan until it thickens. When it thickens, empty it into the *nebet* candy pot with holes. Put the lid on the pot and wrap it in linen sacks. Or bury it in the ground. 1 week later, open the pot and take out the strings and candy.

The Seljuks called candy-sellers *shakar-furush*.

Serves 6.

Flat Kataifi
(Yassı Kadayıf)

For the batter:

5 cups flour

2 cups water

1 cup milk

Iron plate grill

Oil for frying

For the filling:

½ pound walnuts

1 teaspoon cinnamon

5 tablespoons rosewater

For the sherbet:

5 cups sugar

4½ cups water

½ teaspoon powdered essence of lemon

Prepare a soft batter with flour, water, and milk in a deep bowl. Fry ladles of the batter on both sides on an iron plate grill or pan. Brown the walnut kernels in their own oil in another pan. While browning the walnuts, add the cinnamon and rosewater and turn off heat. Put the sugar and water in a deep pot on the stove for the sherbet. When it begins to boil, add the powdered essence of lemon. Boil for 10 minutes and turn off heat. Fill the cakes with the walnut filling and close in the shape of a half moon. Fry the filled cakes in hot oil. Remove the fried cakes from the oil and put them in the sherbet.

Allow the cakes to absorb the sherbet for 10 minutes and serve.

Serves 10.

Almond Candy
(Badem Şekeri)

1 cup almonds

1 cup raw sugar

2 egg whites

¼ teaspoon salt

Crush the sugar in a mortar and put into a broad-base pan. Beat the egg whites and salt in a mixing bowl. Add the almonds to the beaten egg whites. Drain the almonds after they have been dipped into the egg whites. Put the drained almonds into the crushed sugar. Coat the almonds with sugar. When the tandoor is about to go out, put the sugar-coated almonds in the tandoor. (You may bake them in an oven at 150 ºC (302ºF) for 5 minutes.) Spread on a tray to cool. Serve when cooled.

Serves 4 to 6.

Almond Halva

(Badem Helvası)

3 cups almond nuts

Wooden mortar

4 cups rock sugar

Soak the almond nuts in water for 10 minutes. Peel the almonds and put them in the mortar. Grind the almonds until they release their oil and become paste-like. Pour the ground almonds onto a tray. Crush the rock sugar in the mortar until it becomes flour-like and add to the ground almonds. Begin to knead the almonds and sugar. Continue to knead until the ground almonds and sugar take on a doughy consistency. When a dough-like consistency is achieved, serve with a spoon.

Serves 8.

Walnut Halva
(Ceviz Helvası)

3 cups walnut kernels

Wooden mortar

4 cups rock sugar

Crush the walnuts in the mortar until they release their oil and become mushy. Pour the crushed walnuts on a tray. Crush the pieces of sugar in a mortar until they have become like flour and add to the walnuts. Begin to knead the walnuts and sugar. Continue to knead until the walnuts and sugar have become dough-like. When it becomes dough-like, serve the walnut halva with a spoon.

Serves 8.

Sweet Pastry with Walnuts
(Nukul)

2 pound flour

Water as needed

2 tablespoons butter

½ pound walnut kernels

1 cup sugar

1 tablespoon cinnamon

Knead the flour and water into a medium firm dough. Divide the dough into fist-sized balls. Cover the balls of dough with a damp cloth and allow to stand half an hour. While the dough is rising, crush the walnuts in a mortar with sugar and cinnamon. Roll out the balls of dough with a rolling pin to 1/6 inch large rounds. Divide the walnut mixture and sprinkle over rounds. Hold one side of the round and begin to roll it. Cut the rolls into 2 inches slices. Oil a deep copper tray or an oven tray and line up the cut pieces so their fillings can be seen. Repeat with the remaining rounds. Cook the rounds by turning them on top of the stove or until they are browned in the oven. (You may bake them in an oven at 170 ºC (338ºF) for 30 minutes.) Sprinkle with sugar if desired and serve.

Serves 8.

Rice and Saffron Dessert
(Zafiranlı Pirinç Tatlısı)

⅓ cup rice

5 cups water

1 tablespoon corn starch

½ cup water

A pinch of saffron

2 cups sugar

Wash the rice well. Put the washed rice in a medium pan and add 5 cups water. Turn on the heat and bring it to a boil. Melt the corn starch in a half cup water. Wet the saffron with a little water. After boiling the rice for 20 minutes, add sugar, and sieved saffron and corn starch. After boiling another 10 minutes, turn off the heat and pour into bowls. Serve cold.

Serves 8.

Tart Compote
(Mahoş Hoşaf)

1 pound dried plums

1 cup sugar

5 cups water

3 cloves

3 tablespoons sour grape juice

Put the plums, sugar, water, and cloves in a pot. Cook approximately a half an hour. Turn off the heat, add the sour grape juice, and allow to stand. Serve cold.

Since apples, pears, apricots, figs, grapes, pomegranates, and peaches were grown in Anatolia during the time of the Seljuks, we can assume that compote was also made with these fruits.

Serves 6 to 8.

Almond Cookies
(Bure)

1 cup shelled almonds

3 cups flour

½ pound butter

1 cup sugar

Crush the almonds lightly in a mortar. Mix flour, butter and sugar in a deep mixing bowl. Knead until mixture becomes dough-like. Add the almonds to the dough. Break off walnut-sized pieces from the dough and arrange them on an oiled tray. Bake for 25 minutes in a warm tandoor. (You may bake them in an oven at 160 ºC (320ºF) for 25 minutes.) Allow to cool for 15 minutes after removing from tandoor and serve.

There was also Turkmek halva made from honey and almonds in the time of the Seljuks. *Bure* made by using honey instead of sugar and by adding water and browning the mixture was called Turkmek halva.

Serves 6 to 8.

Starch Pudding
(Faluze)

¼ pound wheat starch

3 cups water

1 cup grape molasses

¼ pound walnut kernels

Mix starch and water. Be careful that the starch does not become lumpy. Put the grape molasses and starch water in a medium pan. Turn on the heat and begin to stir and cook. Boil until it thickens and then turn off heat. Pour onto a service dish and sprinkle walnuts on top. Serve cool or warm.

Serves 6 to 8.

Kataifi
(Kadayıf)

3 cups flour

1 cup water

1 cup milk

Iron-plate grill

Copper sieve

3 tablespoons butter

½ pound cream

1 teaspoon cinnamon

3 tablespoons rosewater

3 cups sugar

Make a soft batter with flour, water, and milk. Heat the iron plate grill (or a large pan). Pour the batter over the iron plate with the help of a thin, copper sieve. When the strands of batter begin to brown on the iron plate, transfer them to a tray with the help of a spatula. Repeat for the rest of the batter. When the *kadayıf* strands are ready, add the butter to the tray and put it on the stove. Begin to brown together. When the *kadayıf* turns golden brown, turn off the heat. Spread the *kadayıf* on a service tray and spread cream, cinnamon, rosewater and sugar on top and serve.

Serves 6 to 8.

Türkmek Halva

(Türkmek Helvası)

½ pound butter

2 cups flour

1 cup ground almonds

1 cup honey

2 cups water

Melt the butter in a halva skillet or a large pan. Add the flour and brown without burning. Add the almonds to the browned flour and continue to brown. Add honey and water. Stir faster to avoid cracks. When the halva becomes smooth, turn off the heat and serve.

Serves 6 to 8.

Seljuk glass with bird design (13th century)

- V -
SHERBETS
AND DRINKS

Grape Molasses Sherbet
(Pekmez Şerbeti)

1 cup grape (or any other) molasses
5 cups water

Mix grape molasses and water. Put the mixture in a pitcher. Serve cold.
The Seljuks called sherbet-makers *fukka'i* and water-sellers *sakka*.
Serves 4 to 6.

Pomegranate Sherbet
(Nardenk Şerbeti)

10 large pomegranates
Copper sieve
Clean white muslin cloth
3 cups sugar cubes

Divide the pomegranates down the middle. Empty the pomegranate into a large bowl by hitting the rind with a spoon. Crush the pomegranate pieces in a copper sieve and strain. Strain the pomegranate juice through a clean piece of muslin cloth into a medium pan. Add sugar and turn on heat. Boil until the color turns dark and the juice thickens. Add water after it cools and serve.

Serves 8 to 10.

Vinegar Juice with Honey
(Sirkencubin)

5 cups water

5 tablespoons vinegar

5 tablespoons honey

Mix water, vinegar, and honey in a deep bowl.
Pour into a pitcher, cool and serve.

The Seljuks used ice in their sherbets in the summer.
Ice-sellers were called *mujammid*.

Serves 4 to 6.

Honey Sherbet with Lemon
(Limonlu Bal Şerbeti)

3 lemons

6 cups water

1 cup honey

Grate 3 lemons and squeeze their juice. Boil the lemon juice with 1 cup water in a small pot. Cool the juice for a few minutes and pour it into a pitcher. Add 1 more cup of water and honey. Mix well. Add the remaining water and serve cold.

Serves 6 to 8.

Ayran

1 pound yogurt

2 cups water

½ teaspoon salt

Put the yogurt in a leather bag. Add water and salt. Begin to beat it with a stick. Fat will emerge as it is beaten; put the fat in an earthen bowl. When no fat is left, the rest is *ayran*. Serve cold. (You may make it by the help of a blender, too.)

Serves 4.

Snow Sherbet
(Kar Şerbeti)

3 cups water

2 tablespoons corn starch

2 cups grape molasses

Snow

Mix water and starch in a deep bowl. Strain and pour into a medium pan. Add the grape molasses and boil for 5 minutes. Turn off heat and allow to cool. When you want to make sherbet, dilute the prepared mixture with snow and serve.

I think that the Seljuks ate *karsambaç* or snow and grape molasses. There are records to the effect that this sherbet was made with starch.

Serves 6 to 8.

Rose Sherbet
(Gülap Şerbeti)

10 rose petals

2 cups sugar

1 teaspoon powdered essence of lemon

1 glass jar

Separate the rose petals. Rub the petals with sugar and powdered essence of lemon in a mixing bowl. Put this mixture into a glass jar. Close tightly and put in a window. 15 days later, add water to the rose mixture and serve.

Serves 8.

Grape Sherbet
(Üzüm Şerbeti)

4 pound grapes

Copper sieve

Clean white muslin

Put the grapes in the copper sieve. Place the sieve on a large bowl. Press the grapes with the help of another copper bowl. After the grapes have been pressed, strain them with a white muslin cloth, and empty the grape juice into a pitcher. Serve cold.

Serves 4.

Honey Sherbet
(Bal Şerbeti)

6 cups water

1 cup honey

Warm a cup of water. Mix honey with warm water. Put remaining water in a pitcher and pour the mixture on top. Serve cold.

Serves 4 to 6.

Milk Sherbet

(Süt Şerbeti)

1 cup sugar

1 cup water

5 cups milk

Mix sugar and water in a pan at low heat. When the sugar is melted, turn the heat off. Leave the sherbet cool. Put in a pitcher, and add the milk. Keep it in a refrigerator for 1 hour, and serve.

Serves 4 to 6.

Sugar Sherbet
(Şeker Şerbeti)

1 cup sugar cubes

5 cups water

⅓ cup rosewater

Mix sugar and water. Add rosewater and put in a pitcher.
Keep it in a refrigerator for 1 hour, and serve.

Serves 4 to 6.

Seljuk bowl (13th century)

Seljuk bowl (13th century)